THE CARNEGIE INQUIRY INTO THE THIRD AGE

Research Paper Number 9

HEALTH:
Abilities and Wellbeing in The Third Age

John Grimley Evans, Michael J. Goldacre,
Malcolm Hodkinson, Sallie Lamb and
Margaret Savory

University of Oxford

Published by: The Carnegie United Kingdom Trust
Comely Park House
DUNFERMLINE
Fife KY12 7EJ
for The Carnegie Inquiry into The Third Age

ISBN 0 900259 28 0

FOREWORD

The Carnegie Inquiry into The Third Age was launched by the Carnegie UK Trust in 1990 to consider issues affecting the life, work and livelihood of people who have finished their main job or career, or bringing up their children, or both, but who may have 20 or more years of healthy, active and independent life ahead of them. People enter and leave this stage of their lives at very different ages, and for an individual the transitions may not be clear cut. For statistical purposes we have used the age range of 50-74. This age group is already a quarter of the population of the United Kingdom. Our studies have shown that it is a very diverse group, and whilst many people enjoy great freedom, health and prosperity, others face poverty, isolation and lack of choice; their talents and experience are all too often wasted. Changes of policy, and of attitude, are needed, if the full potential of the third age - for individuals and for society - is to be realised.

Statistics often ignore the third age, grouping 60 year olds with school leavers and healthy 65 year olds with the very old and frail. The Inquiry set out to establish current facts and trends through nine research projects, ranging from large studies of employment, income and learning, to rather more limited work on volunteering, caring, health and homes and travel, and small desk studies of leisure and citizenship. In each case the implications of the research findings have been discussed with policy makers and interest groups, opportunities and areas of concern identified, and policy options suggested. In addition, special work was undertaken on Irish and EC perspectives.

This report is thus one of a series of nine studies intended to fill many of the gaps in current knowledge and launch a public debate on third age policy issues. The views expressed are those of the authors. Drawing on these nine studies, the Advisory Committee (listed on inside back cover) will produce a final Inquiry report setting out their conclusions and recommendations; this will be presented to a major conference in April 1993. This is the EC Year of Older People and Solidarity between Generations.

Mrs Terry Banks
Director, Carnegie Inquiry into The Third Age
November 1992

AUTHOR'S NOTE

This report represents the health study for the Carnegie Inquiry into the Third Age. The authors gratefully acknowledge the support from the Carnegie UK Trust and from the Nuffield Provincial Hospitals Trust who generously funded the health study.

Health can be seen to be a central issue in the third age – the period of life when the imperatives of a full time job and bringing up children recede but when perhaps twenty or more years of healthy, active life lie ahead. Though the third age is essentially a functional life stage, in this report we have generally had to fall back on a chronological definition, equating it to the age range 50 – 74 years.

The report is based on more extensive working papers which were presented at a Health Seminar held in May 1992 at Cumberland Lodge, Windsor Great Park and has gained from the stimulating discussions there. Happily, the more detailed and extensive working papers in their final form are to be published elsewhere thanks to further generous support from the Nuffield Provincial Hospitals Trust for which we are deeply grateful.

We also wish to thank the many individuals and organisations who most generously assisted us in our study. We would also like to give special thanks to Sir Donald Acheson, Dr Michael Ashley-Miller and Dr Hugh Markowe who, as members of the Health Working Group, supported us throughout.

As editor of the report, I would also like to add my personal thanks to Mrs Terry Banks, Director, and Nicholas Rowley, Research Coordinator, at Inquiry headquarters and to my fellow authors who uncomplainingly endured my ruthless shortening of their contributions.

Malcolm Hodkinson

(Emeritus Professor of Geriatric Medicine,University College London)

November 1992

Chiswick

CONTENTS

SUMMARY OF FINDINGS

The findings of our study give considerable ground for optimism regarding health in the third age. It is clear that ageing is not exclusively genetically determined. Even during the third age there is still much that individuals can do to improve their own present and future health and life expectancy.

Mortality has fallen steadily in the third age and it seems likely that both mortality and morbidity will continue to improve if present trends continue and people pursue healthy active lifestyles. However, somewhat paradoxically, our study points to an increase over time in the use of health services, probably reflecting increased expectations rather than increased morbidity but also an increase in the health interventions available. The concept of active life expectancy has been explored as a means of quantifying the gain in non-disabled as opposed to disabled life and holds considerable promise although it is as yet an imperfect tool.

Mental function is crucial to a successful third age and our data indicate that the prevalent pessimistic view that function declines inexorably with age is largely an artefact of cross-sectional studies. Longitudinal studies, whilst showing decline in some individuals, particularly when their physical health deteriorates, generally show good preservation of abilities through the third age. Indeed such functional declines that do occur are often more than adequately counterbalanced by the advantages of increased experience. Thus, for example, older workers may out-perform their juniors and older drivers prove to have a better safety record than the young. Far more positive attitudes to ageing are appropriate and could be put forward more vigorously.

Physical fitness does show substantial declines with age in community samples. This too does not appear to be inevitable but largely to reflect the major diminution in exercise levels in older age groups. There is every indication that an active life style preserves fitness and that appropriate exercise can restore fitness even at older ages. However, we have much to learn as to the most appropriate ways to achieve adequate exercise in those in the third age and much further study could be undertaken. Particularly it could be helpful to know what is effective and safe and yet is acceptable, affordable and enjoyable. Healthy ageing with the preservation of high levels of physical fitness is clearly an achievable goal for those in the third age.

Important causes of mortality in the third age include ischaemic heart disease, stroke, malignant diseases and respiratory disease. Mortality for many of these is already falling in the third age but further progress is likely to be influenced by lifestyle with attention to such risk factors as smoking, alcohol, diet, exercise and blood pressure. These lifestyle!factors appear to act in concert with susceptibility resulting from the quality of nutrition during intra-uterine life and infancy, poor experiences at these periods of life programming the individual to greater risks of high blood pressure, diabetes, ischaemic heart disease and stroke. Though health in the third age reflects earlier lifestyle, changes in the third age can still confer benefits so that, for example, those in the third age who give up smoking reduce their risks of heart disease or bronchitis.

Important causes of disability in the third age include problems with vision and hearing, osteoarthritis, osteoporosis, incontinence, depression and dementia. Prevention is possible for some of these, for example avoidance of occupational trauma and obesity can reduce risks of osteoarthritis whilst exercise may help prevent osteoporosis, falls and fractures. Alternatively, early recognition may enable effective treatment and screening programmes may be justified, for example for hearing disability or for potential causes of loss of vision such as glaucoma. In other cases, for example dementia due to Alzheimer's disease, there is as yet no effective prevention but further research may lead to important future developments.

Policy Options

Available estimates of trends in active life expectancy in later life do not appear to reflect objective changes in health, and probably reflect increasing expectation and aspirations. Government could institute some standard and objective means of monitoring healthy active life expectancy in the population past middle age. This would provide a valuable measure of changes in health status and the likely effectiveness of health and social services and would also give early warning of the advent of unpredicted problems.

The most important single way in which individuals and professionals in the statutory services could add further to the health and well being of people in the third age is undoubtedly to control cigarette smoking. Smoking could be forbidden in all communal areas, tobacco advertising banned and every effort made to increase the real costs of tobacco products.

Throughout both private and public sectors, thought could be given to increasing incentives for healthy behaviour. Among the options are:

(1)   insurance incentives for non-smokers and non- or moderate drinkers could be improved and taxation used to control cigarette and alcohol consumption as far as possible;
(2)   Government and retailers could work together to find ways of developing market practices more conducive to healthy food choice, particularly by those on low incomes. Such initiatives might include modification of pricing structures;
(3)   exercise could be facilitated by discouraging cars from entering urban areas, the provision of more pedestrian precincts and facilitating safer bicycle transport;
(4)   employers could look at further ways to encourage healthy behaviour in the workplace, looking particularly at such issues as smoking, diet, alcohol and exercise.

The media could be encouraged to do more to inculcate healthy lifestyles, particularly among those in the lower socio-economic groups who could most profit. We would not accept the view that the task of the public media is merely to reflect real life to the exclusion of more desirable role models whilst presenting health information in educational programmes mainly watched by higher socio-economic groups. The media should avoid contributing to widening of socio-economic group disparities in health.

Health education efforts could be concentrated on those parts of UK with highest mortality and morbidity rates. However, it is difficult to assess the effectiveness of the various health education initiatives. Some data suggest that health education is improving knowledge without affecting behaviour. Clearly much work could be done on the evaluation of these programmes since they would be a poor investment if they satisfied the conscience of Government without achieving their intended ends.

We welcome the increasing involvement of general practitioners in preventive health care, notably effective in modifying cigarette smoking and alcohol consumption. We would hope to see an increasing orientation towards preventive medicine in both primary and secondary care, involving all members of the health care team. There seems enormous scope for an enhanced role for nurses in this regard.

Prevention appears to have focused mainly on younger adults but there could be the development of training and incentives to bring health care professionals to recognise and implement the potential for preventive action in later life.

Older people are still the victims of many negative stereotypes. Our data show that more positive views could be adopted, towards the older worker or driver for example. Older people are able to benefit from training, if the training is of appropriate design. Exercise can delay or reverse physical declines whilst psychological deterioration with age is not inevitable and is often more than adequately compensated for by knowledge and experience. These positive views could be actively propagated.

Our report points to requirements for further research. We are concerned that research is often under-regarded and perhaps feared by members of the general public. They could be educated to recognise that research is essential to further improvements in health and wellbeing in the third age and that it vitally depends on their volunteering to take part in studies.

Finally, in the interactions between health and lifestyle it is important to recognise that social policies for work, education and activity have important effects on health. The concept of what constitutes the "health budget" could usefully be widened to include employment, housing, education and fiscal policy.

1 DISEASE IN THE THIRD AGE: A PROFILE FROM ROUTINE STATISTICS

1.1 Mortality in the third age

Mortality rates rise exponentially from early adult life, approximately doubling every five years of age in both men and women (figure 1.1). The rates for males are about double those of females at each age.

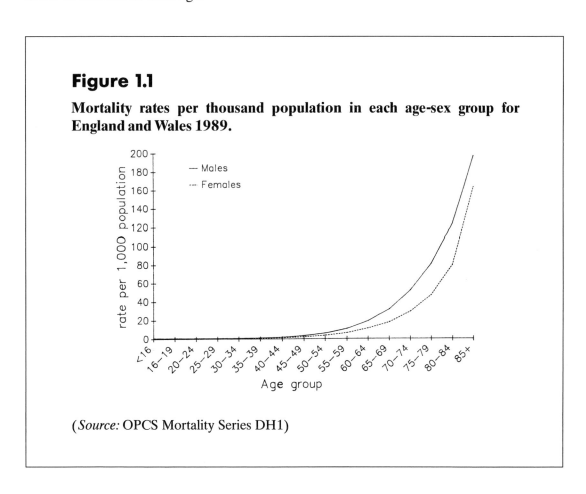

Figure 1.1

Mortality rates per thousand population in each age-sex group for England and Wales 1989.

(*Source:* OPCS Mortality Series DH1)

In males the commonest causes of death in the third age are, in order of frequency, ischaemic heart disease (which includes coronary thrombosis and heart attacks), lung cancer and cerebrovascular disease (strokes). Together, these causes account for just over half of all deaths in the third age. Other common causes of death in males in these age groups include chronic obstructive airways disease (notably chronic bronchitis), cancer of the stomach, large bowel, pancreas, prostate and bladder, leukaemias and lymphomas, and diabetes mellitus. The most common causes of death in females in the third age include cancer of the breast, cancer of the lung, ischaemic heart disease, and cerebrovascular disease. Together, these causes account for just over half of all deaths. Other common causes include cancer of the ovary, stomach and large bowel, chronic obstructive airways disease and diabetes mellitus.

The exponential increase in overall mortality with age is frequently echoed by the pattern for individual causes of death, for example ischaemic heart disease and malignant disease which show higher rates in males and cerebrovascular disease where rates in the two sexes are closely similar. However, not all causes show an exponential pattern, for example motor vehicle traffic accident deaths where there are peaks in young adults of both sexes.

Age-specific mortality rates are higher in Wales, and considerably higher in Scotland and Northern Ireland, than those in England (table 1.1). Age-specific mortality rates in the

Table 1.1

Mortality rates per 10,000 population in England, Wales, Northern Ireland and Scotland.

| | males | | | females | | |
	45-54	55-64	65-74	45-54	55-64	65-74
England	46.7	146.6	391.3	29.5	87.1	224.2
Wales	49.0	159.7	430.9	31.0	91.2	243.7
N Ireland	54.4	172.4	465.8	33.1	95.9	246.7
Scotland	61.3	192.3	484.3	39.2	114.9	246.7

(*Source:* OPCS Mortality Series DH1)

third age have declined over time, as they have in other age groups, since the beginning of the present century (figures 1.2 and 1.3) and proportional decline has been broadly similar in each age group.

Figure 1.2
Changes in age-specific mortality rates in England and Wales for third age men 1911-1985.

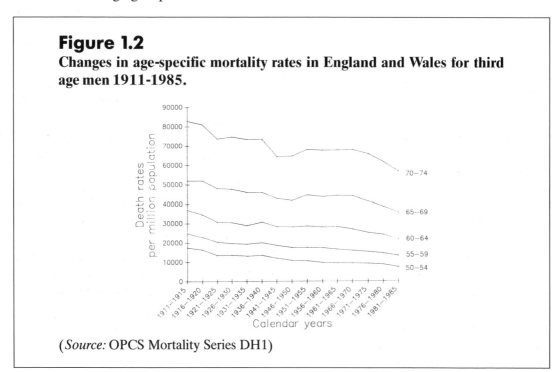

(*Source:* OPCS Mortality Series DH1)

2

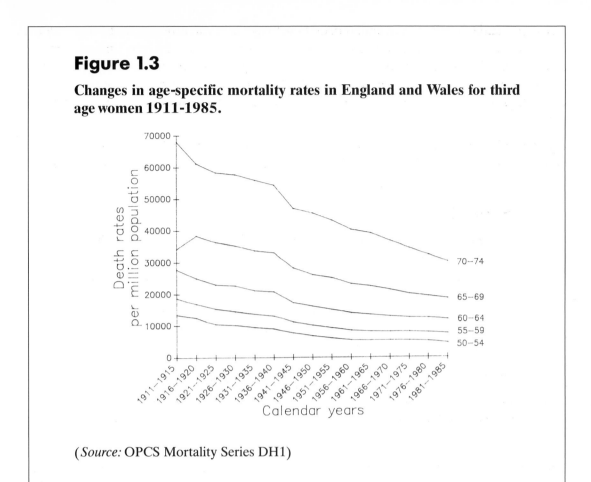

Figure 1.3

Changes in age-specific mortality rates in England and Wales for third age women 1911-1985.

(*Source:* OPCS Mortality Series DH1)

The major component of the decline in mortality in the first half of the century was a reduction in deaths from infectious diseases. Considering individual age groups within the third age, the declines have nonetheless not been entirely smooth over time when considered in detail. For example, in people aged 70-74 years there was a steady decline in death rates for both males and females from the turn of the century until the 1930's. Male death rates then levelled off (figure 1.2) whilst female death rates continued to decline (figure 1.3). Whilst death rates from infectious diseases fell in both sexes, the levelling off of mortality rates in males was due in particular to two major causes of death, lung cancer and ischaemic heart disease, which increased especially in males during this period.

Declines in mortality at a given age and at a given time-period reflect either the influence of the circumstances of that time or the effect of birth cohort (i.e. represent the effect of a generation of healthier people now reaching the relevant age group) or both. These two are difficult to separate out and so it is difficult to predict with precision what future mortality rates may be. We also saw above that trends may be irregular, indicating the dangers of simple extrapolation. However, it seems safe to predict that mortality rates will generally continue to decline, probably substantially. Mortality rates in younger age groups for recent birth cohorts, prior to their reaching the third age, have shown particularly striking declines and presumably the experience of these "healthier" cohorts will continue into the third age.

1.2   Morbidity in the third age – use of health services

1.2.1   Hospital inpatient care

We can compare data for admission rates for hospital inpatient care from two main sources, the Hospital Inpatient Enquiry (HIPE) for England and the Oxford record linkage study. HIPE statistics are episode-based: that is, each hospital admission is counted separately and it is not possible to distinguish between numbers of admissions and numbers of individual people admitted to hospital. In contrast, data from the Oxford record linkage study count each individual once only in the average annual admission rates. Figure 1.4 shows hospital admission rates to all specialties combined for episodes (HIPE). The broad patterns of usage are similar in episode-based and person-based data though admission rates are higher in the former as expected, more so at older ages where multiple admissions are generally more common. Hospital admission rates in adults show little change with age up to about 50 years with higher rates for females than for males, the female excess being accounted for by gynaecological admissions. Thereafter, admission rates rise with age and are somewhat higher in males.

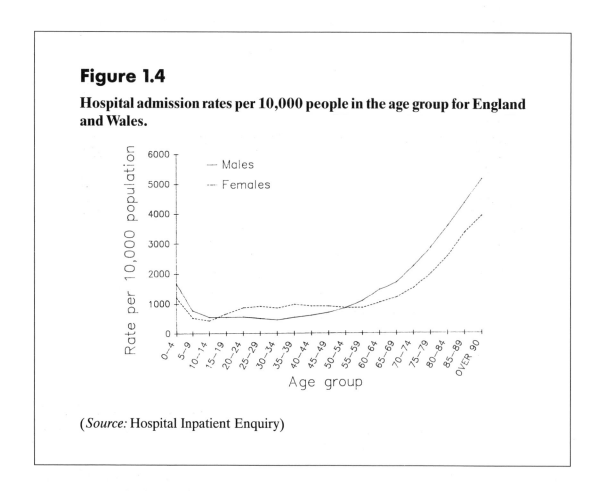

Figure 1.4

Hospital admission rates per 10,000 people in the age group for England and Wales.

(*Source:* Hospital Inpatient Enquiry)

A striking increase in admission rates with age through the third age is seen in the specialties of general medicine, geriatrics, general surgery, trauma and orthopaedic surgery and ophthalmology whilst those in gynaecology decline. There are no striking

4

trends through the third age in admissions to the specialties of ear, nose and throat surgery or dentistry and oral surgery. Admission rates rise and fall across the third age in rheumatology and in radiotherapy. First-ever admission rates to mental illness hospitals show no marked trend but those for presenile and senile dementia show a small increase across the third age. The most common reasons for hospital admission in males and females aged 45-64 and 65-74 years are shown in table 1.2.

Table 1.2

Common reasons for hospital admission with admission rates per 10,000 population.

	men		women
Aged 45-64			
Ischaemic heart disease	58.6	Dilatation & curettage	72.1
Inguinal hernia	42.3	Hysterectomy	41.8
Prostatectomy	15.6	Breast surgery	28.5
Head injury	13.1	Gall bladder disease	17.8
Lung career	12.2	Varicose veins	17.5
Varicose veins	12.1	Back disorders	11.2
Aged 65-74			
Ischaemic heart disease	95.4	Ischaemic heart disease	46.1
Inguinal hernia	63.1	Stroke	32.7
Lung cancer	44.8	Hip arthroplasty	31.4
Stroke	44.2	Lens operations	30.2
Bronchitis	38.2	Breast cancer	29.4
Heart failure	33.6	Heart failure	20.8
Bladder tumours	32.6	Hysterectomy	20.2
Lens operations	27.4	Diabetes mellitus	20.1
Hip arthroplasty	22.0	Gall bladder disease	19.5
Diabetes mellitus	19.9	Femoral fracture	18.2

(*Source:* Oxford Record Linkage Study)

Patients' length of stay in hospital per admission tends to increase with advancing age. Rates of overall bed utilisation, quantified as average numbers of beds occupied daily by people in each age group, also rise with age.

Hospital admission rates have risen for many years in most age groups and in most specialties. Data on the rise in admission rates in general medicine in the third age are illustrated in figure 1.5.

Figure 1.5

Changes in age-specific admission rates for general medicine in Oxford Region 1976-1986.

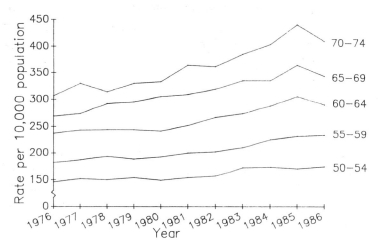

(*Source:* Oxford Record Linkage Study)

1.2.2 Hospital outpatient care

Attendances at hospital outpatient clinics and casualty departments rise with age (table 1.3). However, the increase is not as striking as that seen in either mortality rates or in hospital inpatient admission rates. There has been a gradual increase in outpatient attendance rates over time.

Table 1.3

Percentage of population reporting an outpatient or casualty attendance in previous three months

Year	Males 45-64	Males 65-74	Females 45-74	Females 65-74
1976	10	11	11	11
1979	13	15	13	16
1981	12	14	13	16
1983	13	15	15	18
1985	16	16	15	17
1987	16	17	16	18
1988	14	18	16	17
1989	15	18	17	19

(*Source:* General Household Survey 1989

1.2.3   General practice consultations

Data from the National Morbidity Survey show that episodes of illness resulting in consultation with general practitioners increase with age. This is not as striking as that seen in either mortality rates or hospital admission rates. In this Survey, general practitioners classified illnesses as trivial, intermediate and serious. Consultation rates for episodes of 'severe' and 'intermediate' illness gradually rise through the third age in both sexes. Those for 'trivial' illness slightly increase in males but decrease in females though from a much higher level. General practitioner consultation rates increased by 15-20% from 1971/2 to 1981/2.

1.3   Self-reported illness

The most thorough studies of the prevalence and causes of disability in the UK have been the OPCS disability surveys (Martin, Meltzer and Elliot 1988, Martin, White and Meltzer 1991). They used a complex and sophisticated scheme which graded disability from 1 (least) to 10 (most) and their prevalence rates for these disability levels in the third age are shown in Table 1.4.

Table 1.4

Estimated prevalence of disability as cumulative rates per thousand by disability grade for the age groups 50-59, 60-69 and 70-79.

disability grade	50-59	60-69	70-79
10	2	4	11
9-10	7	16	32
8-10	14	27	57
7-10	22	42	87
6-10	32	57	125
5-10	48	84	169
4-10	64	112	215
3-10	83	143	267
2-10	101	184	332
1-10	133	240	408

(*Source:* Martin, Meltzer and Elliot 1988)

Determination of causes was difficult because of the nature of their survey and because of the complexity of patterns but diagnoses which occurred in 5 or more of disabled adults are listed in Table 1.5.

Table 1.5

Main causes of disability in adults (percentage prevalence in those disabled), England and Wales.

Condition	percentage prevalence
Deafness	32
Arthritis	31
Ischaemic heart disease	8
Chronic Bronchitis	6
Back problems	6
Depression	5
Stroke	5
Cataract	5

(*Source:* Martin, White and Meltzer 1991)

Further information comes from the General Household Survey (OPCS, annual) which records self-reported chronic sickness either as longstanding illness, disability or infirmity or longstanding illness giving rise to limitation of activity. The percentages of people who reported longstanding illness in two serial surveys are shown in figure 1.6. The rates show a gradual increase throughout adult life including the third age. There has been a slight increase over time in the percentage of people reporting longstanding illness in most but not all age-sex groups (figure 1.6) but there has been no corresponding trend for limiting longstanding illness.

Figure 1.6

Percentages of men and women reporting longstanding illness in 1975 and 1989.

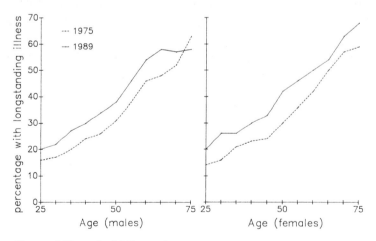

(*Source:* General Household Survey)

In a survey in Oxford Region, the proportions of those reporting their health as being less than 'reasonably healthy' increased with age from 14% aged 45-54 to 18% at 55-64, 20% at 65-69 and 26% at 70-74. Similarly, hearing disability and visual impairment increased whilst ability to walk freely and unaided declined with age (table 1.6).

Table 1.6

Percentages reporting ability to walk about freely, having pain on walking, and hearing or visual disability

age	walking freely	painful walking	hearing disability	visual disability
65-69	73	20	24	17
70-74	60	29	27	22
75-79	50	30	36	26
80-84	35	36	44	36

(*Source:* Oxford Regional Health Authority Health Survey of Elderly People)

1.4   Trends in morbidity and health-care utilisation

The decline in age-specific mortality has not been accompanied by a general decline in health-care utilisation rates. Indeed, increases over time have occurred in hospital admission rates, outpatient attendance rates and general practitioner consultation rates in most age groups. The use of health services depends not only on levels of ill-health but also on levels of provision of services, advances in treatment and care, expectations of individuals for their own health, individuals' thresholds for self-referral, and professional thresholds for referral and use of specialist care. It is therefore difficult, from morbidity statistics based on health-care utilisation alone, to interpret trends over time in utilisation as a reflection of trends in levels of morbidity. In similar ways, self-reported illness may reflect not only absolute levels of morbidity but also individuals' expectations about their health and about the services which may be available to improve it.

2   ACTIVE LIFE EXPECTANCY AND DISABILITY

2.1   The relationship between mortality and morbidity

In the last chapter we saw how age specific mortality rates have fallen over the past century. Marked increases in life expectancy have been seen in almost all countries. Most striking have been the improvements in life expectancy at birth but in the last decade there have also been substantial gains at high ages in many developed countries. However, although the gains in years of life have been clear, there has been controversy over the extent to which the extra years have been achieved by improved health in old age rather than by prolonging the lives of the ill and disabled. Opposing views have been put forward for example by Fries (1980), taking a highly optimistic standpoint, and Gruenberg (1977) expressing a more pessimistic view which has been shared by many recent authors.

2.2   Active life expectancy

This controversy has stimulated the development of measures of active life expectancy (ALE) or expectation of life without disability (ELWD). These have the potential to demonstrate whether the optimistic or pessimistic views are correct, allow comparisons across countries as well as across time which allow for differences in age composition of the populations, and have the potential to be interpreted for individuals. Clearly they could have a useful role in health care planning and monitoring whilst, if their capacity for individual interpretation could be developed, would be of obvious utility in such areas as personal insurance against disability.

Choice of appropriate criteria for transition from active life to dependency is, however, something of a problem. Quality of life measurements or scores summing diagnosed impairments and medical conditions seem inappropriate and functional criteria seem the most suitable. Many studies have thus used criteria based on the concept of limiting long-term illness but results may be very sensitive to alterations in criteria.

Unfortunately criteria have often been dictated by the fact that determination of ALE was not the primary aim of studies; rather data were adapted to this secondary purpose. Better criteria can thus only be expected to emerge in studies specifically designed to investigate ALE and are likely to rely on the activities of daily living (ADL) approach, perhaps with special emphasis on instrumental ADL (ie abilities such as use of a telephone).

Study design may also influence results. Many cross-sectional studies have used data excluding institutionalised people so that assumptions have had to be made about their dependency. Higher ages have often been inadequately sampled and age groupings are often too broad. Serial cross-sectional studies are confounded by cohort differences and these can be substantial. Analysis generally makes two basic assumptions, that disability is irreversible and that mortality is the same in the disabled and the non-disabled; both these assumptions are clearly incorrect. Manton (1988) showed that, even at high levels of impairment, significant proportions showed long-term improvements in function. Similarly correlations of disability with higher mortality have been found in many studies.

As reported figures for ALE from such studies look at the expectations of all subjects, including those already disabled, they seriously underestimate ALE for those who are disability free, particularly for higher ages where initial prevalence of disability is higher. Moreover, as mortality differences are not known, attempts to estimate ALE for the non-disabled will lead to over-estimation given higher mortality of the disabled and the possibility that some disabled subjects have moved to the non-disabled category at follow-up.

Only longitudinal studies can overcome these problems but studies of adequate size have yet to be reported. They will need to avoid excessive loss of individuals at follow-up and fully sample the institutionalised. They must make allowance for reversibility and differential mortality, using for example the multistate analysis of ALE advocated by Rogers, Rogers and Branch (1989).

2.2.1 Reported values for ALE

Females have life expectancy advantages over males at all ages and this is also true for ALE. However the proportion of life expectancy which represents active life is greater for males. This appears to be merely a consequence of the survival advantage of women however for Manton (1988) found no sex differences in the risks of becoming disabled.

Social class differences for ALE appear to be greater than the sex differences. Robine and Richie (1991) showing for pooled international data that if the bottom and top fifths of socioeconomic status are compared, the differences for life expectation and ALE for men are 6.3 and 14.3 years respectively and for women 2.8 and 7.6 years.

Reported values for ALE are closely similar for different developed countries (Bebbington 1988), expectations for England and Wales in 1988 for men and women respectively being 58.5 and 61.2 years at birth and 7.6 and 8.8 years from age 65 (Bebbington 1991).

2.2.2 Changes in ALE with time

Accepting the methodological problems of existing studies, their findings have generally supported the view that increases in life expectancy have not been matched by a proportionate decline in ill-health and disability in later life. Many authors have been quick to draw attention to a variety of effects which might complicate interpretation of these changes. The central problem is that studies generally rely on the individual's perceptions of his own health status. Such perceptions can be shown to be very complex (Blaxter 1990). Thus there are clear sex, age and social class differences whilst other lifestyle variables such as education, occupation, unemployed status and prosperity are also relevant. Katz and colleagues (1983), for example, found lower ALE for the poor compared with the well off. Other writers such as Verbrugge (1984) have considered the impact of changes over time in such things as sickness and disability benefits and diagnostic practice. Clearly better benefits might be expected to make individuals more willing to accept that they are sick or disabled rather than healthy whilst increasing medical diagnosis of such asymptomatic conditions as hypertension and the increasing likelihood that minor long-term illnesses will receive medication means that individuals may be less likely to regard themselves as healthy than they would have been in the past. As Colvez and Blanchet (1981) remarked "the better informed people are, the more limitations they describe".

Two recent set of results are shown in Table 2.1. The study of Crimmins and colleagues (1989) is unusual in that it reports change for a more severe degree of disability, bed disability or long-term institutionalisation, as opposed to the Bebbington study (1991) which, like many others, deals with limiting longstanding illness.

Table 2.1

Changes in expectation of life without disability (ELWD) and expectation of life (EL) in years at birth and at age 65 and the proportion of life gained which is without disability (LGWD).

study & category	ELWD	EL	ELWD	EL	LGWD
United States		1970		1989	
male at birth	65.5	67.0	68.4	70.1	94%
female at birth	72.1	74.6	74.6	77.6	83%
male at 65	12.1	13.0	13.2	14.2	83%
female at 65	15.1	16.8	16.3	18.4	75%
England & Wales		1976		1987	
male at birth	58.2	70.0	58.5	72.4	13%
female at birth	61.7	76.1	61.2	78.1	−25%
male at 65	6.9	12.5	7.6	13.7	58%
female at 65	8.2	16.6	8.8	17.6	60%

(*Sources:* United States, Crimmins and colleagues 1989; England and Wales, Bebbington 1991)

Disability rates appear to have risen in all age groups whilst, according to a pessimistic hypothesis, deterioration ought to be mainly confined to the older age groups where prolonged survival of the chronically ill would have the greatest impact. Indeed, there appear to have been quite substantial gains in ALE in high age groups, these gains forming a *higher* percentage of the increase in total life expectation at 65 than at birth! This strongly suggests that changing expectations in younger age groups may be responsible for the disappointing results for ALE at birth. This interpretation gains support from the very different findings in the Crimmins study as opposed to the Bebbington one, finding more of the gained years were non-disabled when the more stringent and perhaps more objective criterion of bed disability was used. Thus, the pessimistic findings seem more likely to be due to changes in expectations affecting self-reported health status than to any real deterioration in health experience over time.

Clearly we are not seeing the compression of morbidity which Fries hoped for but neither is there clear evidence that longer life is exacting a high price in terms of increased morbidity. The balance of evidence would appear to show that most of the years of life gained are without major disability though there would appear to be a genuine though minor increase in total period of disability. Gains in the length of the third age thus appear to have been considerably greater than those of the fourth age over the last ten or fifteen years in the developed countries and it seems reasonable to anticipate the continuation of these trends.

2.3   The future situation in the third age

2.3.1   Life Expectation

Consistent falls in mortality rates in all age groups including the elderly have been reported from many developed countries. In England and Wales for the period 1968-85 (OPCS 1991), mortality rates for ages 50-75 fell by an average of 0.9% per year in women and 1.3% per year in men. It seems reasonable to expect these consistent trends to be maintained at least in the short and medium term. Projection from this OPCS data leads to estimates of survival to age 75 from age 50 of 74% for women and 59% for men in the year 2000, representing gains of 10% and 28% respectively on expectations in 1975 (table 2.2).

Table 2.2

Survival and survival without disability from aged 50 in females and males.

Age	% survial		% survival without disability	
	female	male	female	male
55	98.3	97.8	95.0	94.6
60	94.5	91.7	87.0	84.5
65	88.6	82.1	76.3	70.7
70	81.2	70.1	63.4	54.8
75	72.7	57.2	49.0	38.5

2.3.2   Disability

Trends for disability, as already discussed, are far less clear cut. Many social, attitudinal, environmental and medical changes may influence self-reported disability rates favourably or adversely and can be broadly expected to cancel out. Recent estimates of disability rates are therefore the best estimates for the medium term future. Estimates taking OPCS data for any disability and combining these with survival data estimated for year 2000 lead to the estimates for disability-free survival shown in table 2.2. The estimate is that a non-disabled man of 50 would have a 39% chance of surviving in the non-disabled state to the age of 75 whilst a woman would have a 49% chance.

3   PSYCHOLOGICAL CHANGES IN THE THIRD AGE

3.1   Age-associated changes

Psychological processes are important in determining a person's ability to interact with and respond to the environment. General well-being and the pursuit of an active independent lifestyle depend as much on the maintenance of cognitive function as on the maintenance of physical health. What then are the changes in psychological function that occur in the third age? An important question is whether changes in cognitive functioning are an unavoidable consequence of aging. Pessimistic views have largely come from cross-sectional studies but their findings are confounded by cohort, period and illness effects (Schaie 1988).

Cohort effects seem relevant for there is evidence of generational shifts in performance on standard intelligence tests. Flynn (1984, 1987) reported a trend towards increased IQs in successive generations in fourteen nations including the UK. Lynn and Hampson (1986) reviewed eleven studies of British children and reported a net increase of 1.71 IQ points per decade since the 1930s. A consequence of this generation effect is that, in a cross-sectional study of IQ and age, young people will inevitably achieve better average scores than the old. Such 'cohort effects', if unrecognised, can lead to a distorted estimate of the impact of age on mental function. Unbiased measures of age-associated changes can only be obtained by assessing individuals against their own performance at earlier ages.

3.1.1   Health effects

Two alternative models of cognitive aging have been proposed, continuous decline and terminal drop (figure 3.1). The former models the changes found in numerous cross-

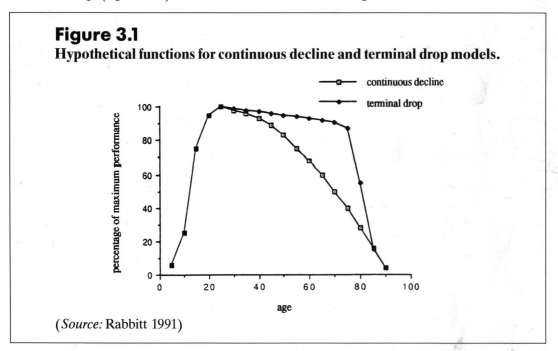

Figure 3.1

Hypothetical functions for continuous decline and terminal drop models.

(*Source:* Rabbitt 1991)

14

sectional studies, a gradual decline from a peak in middle age, whereas the more optimistic terminal drop model suggests that any decline is associated with some underlying pathology, rather than as a result of age alone. Evidence for "terminal drop" comes from longitudinal studies showing that many individuals are able to maintain cognitive abilities provided that physical health is also maintained (eg Schaie 1990). Cross-sectional data cannot distinguish between these two alternatives. Longitudinal studies are essential but these are time-consuming (obviously), difficult to run, and have their own methodological shortfalls (Rabbitt 1983).

Rabbitt and colleagues at the University of Manchester have established large-scale studies, involving hundreds rather than tens of subjects, and are among the first to provide comprehensive profiles of cognitive function in ageing in UK. A recent survey of a nationally representative sample (The Health and Lifestyle Survey, Huppert 1987) included psychological measures. Most longitudinal data, however, have been derived from studies conducted in the USA.

3.1.2   Intellectual Abilities

Cross-sectional studies have generally pointed to a decline in intellectual functioning after a peak in young adulthood. However, such decline is not universal for all aspects of intelligence. A "classic ageing pattern" has been demonstrated by many studies where tests of verbal ability (including vocabulary) remain stable over the lifespan, whereas non-verbal tasks show a steady decline. Results from longitudinal studies challenge "the myth of intellectual decline" (Schaie 1974) typically finding abilities on most tests holding up well over the years and any declines found starting later than cross-sectional studies suggest. Thus, for example, Schaie and Strother (1968) found that a composite score of verbal and reasoning ability showed increments to age 55. Furthermore, the estimated score at 75 years was still above that at 25.

The longitudinal design can be improved by a cross-sequential strategy, consisting of repeated longitudinal and cross-sectional sampling from the same population: several birth cohorts being examined over the same chronological age period. The Seattle Longitudinal Study (Schaie 1990) used this design and found performance improved until 40-50, whilst deterioration was not evident until the late sixties and then not for everyone. Indeed, between 75 and 85 were able to maintain levels of performance on specific intellectual tests over a 7 year period at age 60 and even at age 81 the proportion remained around 60 and few individuals showed a universal decline on all aspects of their mental abilities.

Thus, intellectual decline is not an inescapable consequence of ageing for all individuals. For some, there may be a decrement of some (but not necessarily all) abilities in their sixties, but for others it will be even later, and in others not at all. Many enter advanced old age still performing at the level of younger adults. Certainly in the period of the third age, most individuals will still be functioning at or near their peak levels.

3.1.3   Memory

Memory can be considered as consisting of short-term and long-term memory. Short-term memory is considered to be a limited capacity store, a temporary repository of information before it passes to the unlimited, permanent, long-term memory. Several studies have found little or no age-associated loss in short-term memory (Craik 1977). Larger age differences have been found for long-term memory, as exemplified by the free recall of word lists, eg the Health and Lifestyle Survey (Huppert 1987). However, there was overlap between the age groups and men showed a greater decline than women (figure 3.2). Rabbitt (1992) also found an increased likelihood of lower scores with age, though substantial numbers still retained their memory ability.

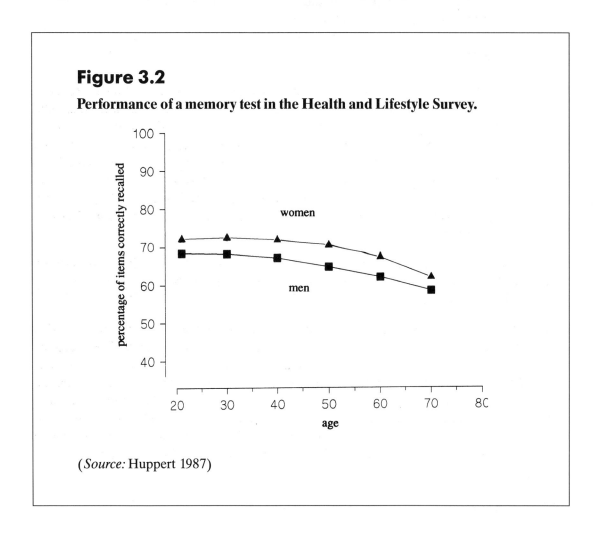

Figure 3.2

Performance of a memory test in the Health and Lifestyle Survey.

(*Source:* Huppert 1987)

3.1.4   Reaction Speed

With increasing age reaction speed becomes slower but the changes reported from cross-sectional studies tend to be larger than those from longitudinal studies (Schaie and Strother 1968). Reaction times can be divided into a central "decision component", the time taken to process the information and decide what response to take, and a peripheral "motor" component, the time taken to execute the appropriate response. With increased age the changes in central processes are greater (Krauss 1987, Salthouse 1985, Cerella 1985).

Slowing of reaction times has been demonstrated on a variety of tasks but decrements are greater for complex tasks, the response speed of an older person (say aged 70) being approximately one and a half to twice as long as a person of 20-30. Wilkinson and Allison (1989) found large variations in reaction time within age groups; in each age group there were people who were faster than others in lower age groups. Similar results were found in The Health and Lifestyle Survey (Huppert 1987).

Schaie (1988) observed samples to determine whether the slowing of reaction time in older individuals had a disabling impact on their occupational pursuits and concluded that it did not. It was virtually impossible to detect activities where increases in reaction time in fractions of seconds were at all relevant.

3.1.5 Attention

Attention, defined as the capacity to support cognitive processes, is a limited capacity system and can be divided into selective attention, divided attention and sustained attention (or vigilance), although they are not necessarily independent. Selective attention is needed for efficient goal-directed behaviour, filtering out irrelevant and focusing on relevant available information. Rabbitt (1965) suggested an age-associated decline in the ability to ignore irrelevant information. This has been confirmed by other studies but difficulties may only be apparent when a search task is particularly effortful and may lie in discrimination between relevant and irrelevant, rather than in ability to ignore the irrelevant.

Divided attention is necessary to perform two tasks concurrently but with equal success. Several studies have shown that older adults perform less well but task complexity may be an important influence.

Sustained attention is needed to maintain performance on a task over an extended period of time. The ability of the old to sustain attention depends on type of task and the aspect of performance measured. Davies and Parasuraman (1982) reported that only half of the studies they reviewed found a significant age effect, showing older groups (60 or over) to be disadvantaged. However, older people may show less confidence and therefore adopt more rigorous response criteria than younger people. Age-associated differences in cognitive processing may be accounted for by differences in the speed with which the brain processes information but this may not always be the dominant factor (Salthouse 1985).

3.2 Compensatory effects of experience and skill

Experience and expertise appear to counteract any potential adverse effects of age on performance in everyday activities. Salthouse (1990) contrasts cognitive ability, the individual's intellectual test level, with cognitive competence, the use of abilities to adapt to the particular situation. We should note that, in general, laboratory tests investigate ability, whereas real-life requires competence.

3.2.1 Work Performance

The stereotype that the older worker is less competent and productive persists though evidence of changed performance with age is at best "mixed". In a review of 25 empirical studies conducted over the last 30 years, Rhodes (1983) found that there were studies showing improvement, deterioration or no change with age! She concluded that the age-performance relationships observed depended on the performance measure used, the demands and nature of the job and on individual experience. Giniger and colleagues (1983) looked at productivity for jobs using "speed" or "skill" in garment workers. For skill jobs there was a steady improvement in productivity with age whilst for speed jobs, performance only declined at the highest ages (figure 3.3). In a study of typists (age range 19 to 72 years), Salthouse (1984) found that, although reaction time tests increased significantly with age speed of copy typing remained constant across age groups. Furthermore, maintained speed was not at the expense of accuracy, as older typists also made fewer errors.

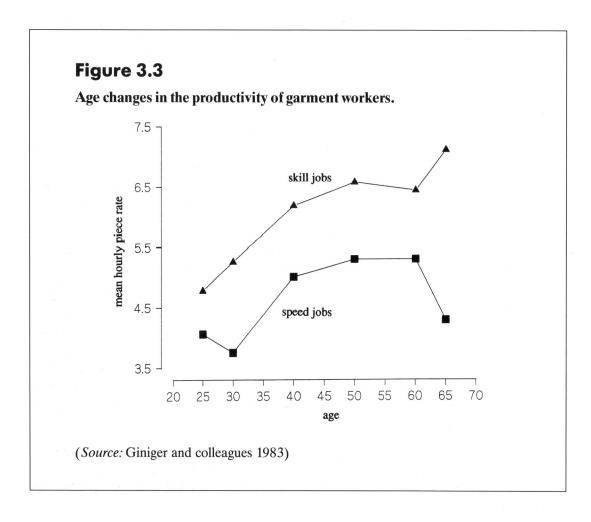

Figure 3.3

Age changes in the productivity of garment workers.

(*Source:* Giniger and colleagues 1983)

The importance of experience in overcoming declines in ability is emphasised by these studies. As Davies, Matthews and Wong (1991) say, "Overall, however, no clear evidence emerges of a universal age deficit in job performance, although older workers may be disadvantaged in particular kinds of jobs, for example those requiring physical strength, speeded reactions, or close attention to visual detail. The range of performance variation is considerable, probably more so among older than among younger workers, and in many cases older workers seem able to perform at least as well as, and sometimes better than, younger colleagues". However, older workers may be at a disadvantage in novel situations, where there is little or no experience to call upon.

18

3.3 Capacity for learning and improvement

Many experiments may not truly reflect capabilities of the older person, as they often involve minimal amounts of practice. Experimental reports consistently show that, given the opportunity to practice, older persons can improve their performance to a greater extent than the young and reduce though not eliminate the age deficit. Transferability of practice may depend on similarity of tasks; Hoyer and colleagues (1978) found no carry over of practice effect from a reaction time task to an intelligence task that involved speed of response whilst Menich and Baron (1990) found successful transfer from a visual to an similar auditory recognition memory task.

Thus, older people are able to learn so that, even if cognitive performance has deteriorated, there is scope for the decline to be reversed. This has been demonstrated with skills training (Hill and colleagues 1990, Schaie and Willis 1986).

3.3.1 Training for Work

As older individuals can learn new tasks and improve performance with practice they are, therefore, equally likely to benefit from training. Although still versatile and capable, they may have different needs from younger workers. Older workers are liable to be disadvantaged in training and retraining if the methods used to train younger workers are applied without modification. Training programmes need to recognise their specific requirements.

The results from several studies have suggested a number of features that should be incorporated into training programmes in order to benefit older persons:

(1)   A fast pace, for either presentation or recall, handicaps the older learner but, if allowed to work at their own chosen speed, their performance can equal that of younger individuals. Written instructions may be of greater value than lectures. Similarly, a video may be preferable to a demonstration, because it can be repeated or run slowly. Given appropriate pacing, older workers do learn effectively as has been shown for driver retraining (Shooter and colleagues 1956), use of a software package (Zandri and Charness 1989) and training for word processing (Elias and colleagues 1987) for example.

(2)   As older adults tend to be less successful at recall than younger adults, training that avoids unnecessary memorisation may be advantageous, Belbin (1958) showing that older subjects improved their performance if they learned a task through activity rather than memorisation.

(3)   Errors early in training should be prevented as Kay (1951) noted that, in terms of learning a serial task, subjects in their fifties and sixties were both slower and less accurate. After learning an initial task, subjects were required to learn a similar task, but with serial positions changed. Older subjects persisted with errors made in earlier trials perhaps because they found patterns of responses more difficult to modify.

(4)   Welford (1976) suggests that the performance of older people depends upon their capacities but also on their attitudes and motivation. Though not unwilling, older people can be more hesitant to commit themselves to action, or more cautious, gathering

more information before making decisions. Other factors to hinder performance may be fear of failure, or having to "compete" against younger trainees, perhaps with higher educational attainments. In order to maintain a person's confidence, it is important that positive feedback is provided.

(5)   The discovery method of training is a synthesis of many of the above points and has often been found superior to conventional methods of training for both young and older workers (Welford 1988). Those undergoing training are given a minimum of instruction and then allowed to discover for themselves how the task is to be completed, in controlled circumstances where they are required to make active decisions, and any errors are immediately corrected. Such methods may require higher levels of input by the trainers, but the obvious reward is the greater success for the older trainee.

3.4   Driving

The ability to drive is often important for independence at any age, but perhaps particularly as one becomes older. In a survey of one thousand drivers over the age of 55 years, more than three-quarters of respondents felt that, in overall terms, having a car was essential or very important to their way of life (AA Foundation 1988).

As driving is a complex task which relies heavily on both visual information processing and speed of reaction, it is often assumed that driving performance deteriorates with age, given the large body of evidence pointing to declines in psychological function. However, as Rabbitt (1991a) points out "although all these, and many other, pessimistic conclusions from laboratory experiments must be taken seriously, they all derive from very small-scale studies and so allow us to make only very limited generalisations about the abilities of the entire elderly population. They must therefore be taken only as useful indicators of possible trends of age-related competence in the real world, and as stimuli for devising help and remediation, rather than as excuses for Procrustean legislation to curtail the rights of elderly road users."

3.4.1   Accident Data

Most recent statistics indicate that actual driver casualty rates decrease with age (Road Accidents of Great Britain 1990, table 3.1). However, this information is of limited value in determining driving performance in that the likelihood of being injured may increase with age and travel survey data indicate that older drivers travel less than does the "average" driver. When distance travelled is taken into account, accident and casualty rates are relatively high among young drivers, start to fall with age, then rise again. UK statistics for 1986 show that this rise starts to occur between 60-65 years of age, with slight differences for males and females (Broughton 1987, table 3.2). However, it is only above the age of 74 that the highest rates are observed. Accident rates for both men and women between the ages of 69 and 73 are still lower than for drivers up to the early thirties. Furthermore, the observed upturn in accident rates for older drivers may be an exaggeration. Those with lower mileage tend to accumulate this in a higher risk urban environment whereas high-mileage drivers, usually younger, gain most miles on motorways, where the driving task is less complex and the accident rate per distance travelled is lower.

Table 3.1

Casualty rates per 100,000 population showing those killed, totals for those killed or seriously injured (KSI) and injuries of any degree of severity (IAS).

age	car drivers			car passengers		
	Killed	KSI	IAS	Killed	KSI	IAS
17-19	6.9	97	610	6.7	88	505
20-29	5.1	67	449	2.8	34	223
30-39	2.8	40	287	0.8	15	101
40-49	2.3	30	210	1.0	12	82
50-59	2.2	25	161	0.8	12	83
60-69	2.1	19	100	1.2	13	78
70+	2.7	17	72	2.2	14	70

(*Source:* Road Accidents of Gt Britain 1990)

Table 3.2

Accident rates per 100 million vehicle kilometres for car drivers by sex and age, Great Britain 1986.

Age	Males	Females
17-20	440	240
21-24	180	180
25-28	140	140
29-33	104	135
34-38	83	105
39-43	80	104
44-48	70	84
49-53	64	91
54-58	61	76
59-63	68	100
64-68	83	110
69-73	96	130
74+	170	360

(*Source:* Road Accidents of Great Britain 1987)

Thus, although the increase in accident rates amongst older drivers is a cause for concern, it should not be used as a reason for discrimination. Indeed, if accident rates were the sole criterion for deciding which age groups are safe to drive, then, perhaps, it would be the younger driver who would be excluded! Analysis of accident data, however, has proved useful in indicating that older and younger drivers differ in the accidents to which they are prone. Whereas young drivers are more frequently involved in accidents caused by speeding, older drivers are more prone to intersection-related driving errors, such as turning and yielding right of way. These situations are usually more complex, but occur at lower speeds. Accidents involving laterally moving vehicles or attentional deficits (disobeying traffic signals etc) tend to increase with age. Conversely, following and skidding accidents appear to decrease with age, probably related to the decreasing inclination to drive at high speed.

3.4.2 Self-Reported Driving Experiences

Questionnaire-based surveys (eg Cooper 1990) show that older drivers recognise some areas of difficulty and modify their behaviour accordingly, usually by avoiding that situation. In particular, older drivers appear to be concerned by visual problems and tend to avoid driving at night when visual deficits become most pronounced. Rabbitt (1991a) found that accident rates proved to be lower amongst those who had altered their driving behaviour because of noticing a change in their sensory abilities. Specific problems apart, many older drivers perceive that they have altered their approach to driving. In the AA survey, when asked about changes since aged 50, only 19 reported no changes overall. In particular, drivers asserted that they left more distance from the vehicle in front and were more cautious. These views were more apparent in those over 65 than in those 55-64. However, older persons are not necessarily aware of all their areas of difficulty, pointing to a greater need for re-education and feedback.

3.4.3 Visual Abilities

Vision plays a crucial role in driving processes but the relationship between visual abilities and driving performance is unclear. Vision is just one of many factors affecting driving and most visual tests are not geared specifically to the driving situation and their direct relevance may be questioned. There are no clear correlations between poor visual acuity and high accident rates for drivers aged under the mid fifties. For those older than mid-fifties, a weak relationship between dynamic and static visual acuity and accident rates has been found. Given the major effects of poor illumination on acuity in older age groups, improvements in road lighting might be of particular benefit to older drivers. Peripheral visual field loss is another important consequence of aging and this may contribute to the problems experienced by older drivers at junctions. However, age associated deterioration in attention might also be relevant.

3.4.4 Reaction Speed

As already indicated, with increasing age reaction speed becomes slower, particularly for complex tasks. There is evidence that older subjects are less sensitive to velocity changes than are younger subjects. This may be relevant to driving where decisions about relative velocity of other vehicles are of paramount importance (Brown and Bowman, 1987).

However, speed of reaction has not been directly related to driving performance; pessimistic conclusions concerning the older driver's ability to react quickly in traffic are unjustified. In fact, field studies indicate that reaction speed does not affect speed of response in the driving situation; a further example of practice and experience counteracting difficulties caused by diminished abilities. Indeed, in a comparison of healthy young and older drivers on a standardised road test, the older group were found to have superior driving skills and made fewer errors (Carr and colleagues 1992).

3.5   Conclusion

Perhaps the greatest barriers to an active and independent life in the third age are not a person's abilities but negative stereotypes and sweeping generalisations. Like younger individuals, older individuals are a heterogeneous group and should be so considered.

4 PHYSICAL FITNESS AND THE IMPORTANCE OF EXERCISE IN THE THIRD AGE

Although intrinsic processes of ageing result in a decrease in physical fitness or capacity for physical work, other factors are also responsible (Edwards and Larson 1992), most importantly a sedentary lifestyle (Bassey 1978). A growing consensus of opinion points to the significant role that exercise has in the maintenance of physical and mental health and functional ability in the third age and beyond (Edwards and Larson 1992). Despite this, the fitness of many individuals in the third age, and their participation in conditioning activities, is below that required to ensure good functioning in daily life (National Fitness Survey 1992).

4.1 Age-associated changes in physical fitness, and their importance in everyday life

Physical fitness is essentially dependent on the integrated action of four attributes – stamina, strength, suppleness and skill. A universal phenomenon of ageing is a decline in each of these attributes, which eventually results in a loss of fitness. Although some of these age-associated changes do appear to be attributable to intrinsic ageing processes, there is considerable individual variation in the rate and extent of decline. This suggests that the decline is also dependent on a number of other factors, including co-existent medical illness, smoking, poor nutrition, and low levels of exercise (Edwards and Larson 1992).

Many simple everyday activities require a minimum threshold of fitness for their completion so that the body has to be sufficiently physically conditioned if it is to meet the challenges of ordinary life. A model which demonstrates the importance of maintaining fitness in older age is shown in figure 4.1 (Young 1986). A healthy 20 year old subject will require only 50-70% of their strength to rise from a low armless chair, but a healthy 80 year old female must make a maximal effort. Reserve capacity is lost and fitness falls to a critical "threshold" level so that any further decline jeopardises independence. If a subject has a lower fitness level for his age, the ability to stand up will be compromised earlier whilst, if fitness is high, performance can be sustained to a greater age, emphasising the fact that reduced fitness and poor performance in activities of daily living are not an inevitable consequence of ageing.

4.2 Age-associated changes in strength

There is a well documented loss of muscle strength, power and mass with increasing age. The decline in mass is the effect of a gradual reduction in the number of muscle fibres which begins at birth. The resultant loss of strength and power is accelerated from the age of 60 years onwards by a selective atrophy of stronger muscle fibres and decrease in innervation. As a consequence, the strength (averaged over all muscle groups) of subjects aged over 70 years, is at least 20% less than that of young adults. Importantly, evidence suggests that when customary activity is maintained, so is strength, despite increasing age (Bassey 1978, Bassey and colleagues 1988).

Lower limb muscles, notably the Quadriceps muscle, are particularly important in activities of daily living such as walking and climbing stairs, rising from a chair, and in maintaining balance. Quadriceps is particularly vulnerable to age-associated loss of strength from the fifth decade onwards.

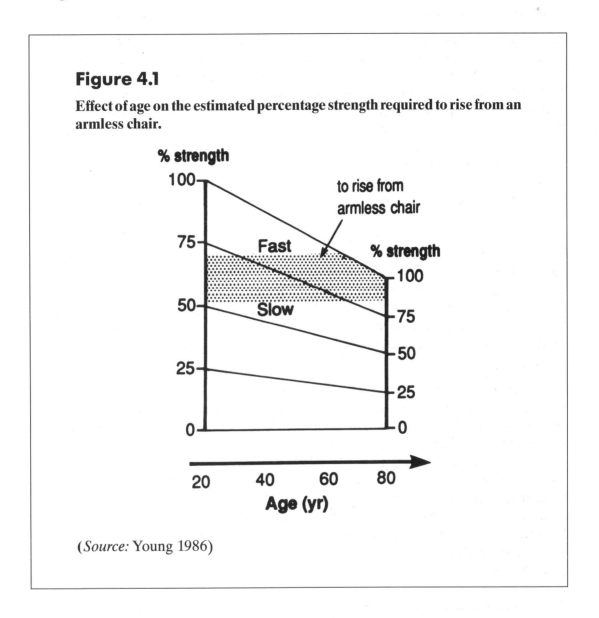

Figure 4.1

Effect of age on the estimated percentage strength required to rise from an armless chair.

(*Source:* Young 1986)

Upper limb strength is essential for manual dexterity, and ability to wash, dress and feed oneself. Loss of hand grip strength has been shown to correlate positively with dependent living (Williams 1984, 1987).

Muscle power determines how quickly strength can be generated, and appears to be much more sensitive to age-associated decline. Upper limb power output fades from about 40 years of age, whereas strength fades from 60 years onwards. Leg extensor power is important for walking, climbing and rising from a chair, and a threshold power of 0.5 Watts/kg of body weight has been suggested as essential for activities of daily living (Bassey and colleagues 1992). A recent report suggests a rate of decline in leg extensor power of 3.5% per annum in healthy men and 3.7% per annum in healthy women between the ages of 65-84 years (Skelton and colleagues 1992). Encouragingly, loss of strength and power can be minimised by regular physical activity (Edwards and Larson 1992, Bassey and colleagues 1992).

4.3 Age-associated changes in stamina

Stamina, or ability to sustain activity, is dependent on the rate at which oxygen can be delivered to the working tissues and the ability of tissues to extract and utilise oxygen. Stamina decreases by up to 10% per decade over middle life regardless of habitual activity level but the underlying mechanisms are not clearly understood. Possible explanations include a decreased ability to utilise oxygen caused by changes in cellular enzymes or, more likely, as a consequence of a reduced muscle mass. A decrease in the ability of the circulation to transport oxygen cannot be excluded as ageing affects the structure and function of the heart, major vessels and lungs. These age changes include a decrease in vascular distensibility, associated with an increase in blood pressure, and the heart valves become thicker and more rigid.

Changes in connective tissue decrease lung compliance whilst stiffness of the chest wall increases and respiratory muscle strength decreases with age, the combined effect of which is a reduction in lung capacity. This loss of lung capacity is thought only to affect stamina in the older old, or in situations where the lungs have been subjected to additional insults such as smoking.

A reduction in stamina means that a task will require a greater effort to ensure completion. Certain activities may become unpleasant, or even impossible to perform. Decreased muscle strength and joint suppleness, which are commonly observed in older people, also increase the stamina required to complete a task.

Stamina affects quality of life in many situations. Some occupations demand considerable stamina, as do heavy household chores and some leisure pursuits. Consequently, if a person wishes to lead an active independent life, stamina is an essential pre-requisite. The age-associated decline in stamina is accelerated by sedentary habits, the presence of heart disease or smoking, emphasising the importance of a healthy lifestyle.

4.4 Age-associated changes in skill

The contribution of the central nervous system to fitness and ability in activities of daily living, might not at first seem apparent. However, the completion of any task requires skill, a characteristic of predominantly central nervous system origin. Motivation is also important. The integrity of the central nervous system is essential to avoid falls and accidents; loss of cells in the brain stem and cerebellum and diminution of peripheral proprioceptive function limit the co-ordination of body movements, including the correction of externally imposed forces. An increased movement and reaction time, an alteration in the central processing of information and deterioration in vision and hearing also contribute to age-associated decline in skill.

4.5   Age-associated changes in suppleness

Connective tissue undergoes histochemical and structural change with advancing age. These changes are not restricted to joints alone; tendons, ligaments and muscles are also affected. Muscle stiffness is common as muscles become more susceptible to fatigue. The ability to recover from minor sprains and strains is lessened, perhaps because of a reduction in blood supply to the soft tissues or because of decreased activity levels. Osteoarthritis is common in older age groups and the loss of mobility and instability increases the absolute energy cost of activities of daily living. Osteoarthritis can also lead to a painful restriction of movement. Self care ability, for example dressing, may be limited if range of movement in the shoulders is restricted. If the lower limbs are affected there may be a serious impairment of gait. Loss of suppleness in the hip may cause limping, and difficulty in performing some of the key activities of daily living such as climbing stairs, getting out of a bath and rising from a low chair. Involvement of the knee also causes difficulty in stair climbing.

4.6   The importance of exercise

Regular exercise is fundamental to the maintenance of physical fitness at any age. This is demonstrated by the profound detrimental effect that immobilisation has on both young and older people. Individuals who exercise regularly throughout their lives tend to maintain a higher level of function and experience less decline in functional status than sedentary individuals (Edwards and Larson 1992).

Encouragingly, recent research suggests that appropriate exercise benefits even sedentary elderly persons who begin exercise at an advanced age (Edwards and Larson 1992). Benefits include increased muscle strength and power, increased stamina and increased joint suppleness. Exercise may also slow or prevent some of the intellectual and psychomotor decline which is associated with ageing, although further research is required to confirm this (Edwards and Larson 1992).

Despite a growing consensus of opinion that exercise of appropriate intensity may benefit older persons, participation in conditioning exercise remains low. Whether this is because the general public does not realise the potential benefits of exercise or what constitutes appropriate or conditioning exercise, or that exercise is not being incorporated into care programmes by health professionals are issues of great importance.

4.7   How much, and what type of exercise do we need to maintain or regain fitness?

A training effect will only occur if exercise is of an "appropriate" intensity, duration, frequency and nature. However, what constitutes "appropriate" is a contentious issue, and a source of confusion to both those giving and taking advice. There has been minimal study of the exercise prescription required to ensure functional fitness in the third age, a difficult area given the heterogenous nature of the people in this age group. However, some authors have devised guidelines based on available research, but these have to be interpreted with some caution as they usually refer to healthy younger people. When deciding on suitable exercise regimes careful consideration must be given to four factors – safety, effectiveness, enjoyment and cost.

4.7.1 Safety

It is a common belief that exercise carries an increased risk of a cardiac event. On the contrary, data indicate that the risk of a cardiac event while taking exercise is relatively low in the 50-69 year old age group (Vouri and colleagues 1982). However erratic participation in vigorous activity by sedentary individuals does carry a high risk. Musculo-skeletal injury occurs when the demand of an exercise regime has been too great, when there has been little or no "warming up and down", poor attention to the flooring and lighting in the environment, or poor choice of footwear. Obesity increases the risk of injury (Shephard 1987).

Individuals who are worried about their health and ability to undertake regular exercise should seek advice from their general practitioner, practice nurse or physiotherapist. This raises the issue that health professionals must be adequately trained to give appropriate advice.

4.7.2 Effectiveness

In order to maximise functional ability of elderly people, a general training regime which utilises specific exercise for stamina, skill, suppleness and strength is required. These exercises must be of sufficient intensity, duration and frequency if they are to have a beneficial effect. Concern over safety is often so great that exercise levels are moderated to a point where they are no longer effective (Shephard 1987). However there are few complications associated with increasing activity, and, thus exercise should be regarded as safe for most individuals (Edwards and Larson 1992).

Daily activity is essential to keeping fit. People should endeavour to walk for at least sixty minutes a day (Astrand 1986). This need not be continuous, and can include moving, walking, and climbing the stairs. This should be interspersed with periods of greater activity designed to build up stamina. Stamina is increased in situations where heart rate is significantly increased, to between 120-150 beats per minute depending on initial fitness (Shephard 1987). Two or three weekly sessions of brisk walking, swimming or similar activity, sustained for a period of 20-30 minutes, would fulfil this requirement (Astrand 1986). These activities are also considered to be sufficient to maintain strength in the legs of an older person (Shephard 1987). Isometric muscle contractions are useful for strengthening muscles which are especially weak, as long as they are not held against heavy resistance, and are not sustained for too long (Shephard 1987). Weight lifting, or sustained efforts are not considered safe in older persons as the exertion produces significant changes in blood pressure (Shephard 1987). Suppleness can be improved by simple stretching exercises. Of special importance are the shoulders, hips, knees and ankles. Simple exercises in which a stretch is maintained at the end of range, should be sufficient. Skill must be considered when prescribing exercise as it may predispose to injury if compromised. Therefore, exercises should be simple in the initial stages of training and, with increased fitness, progress to more complex tasks.

These guidelines are appropriate for a healthy person in the third age though the more frail or unfit need a regime which gradually builds up fitness. People who have impairments such as stroke or diabetes should consult an exercise specialist for individual advice and prescription. Older people should be advised to exercise to a degree that produces no more than a pleasant tiredness (Shephard 1987). If they do experience tightness or excessive pounding of the chest they should stop exercising and seek professional advice (Shephard 1987).

4.7.3   Enjoyment

To ensure motivation and compliance with an exercise programme an older person must both enjoy the experience and be able to identify gains in health and fitness (Shephard 1987). Hobbies or interests that people currently enjoy, or have had previous experience with, can often be exploited. So for example, bowls, ballroom dancing or golf may be more attractive to an individual, but as effective as swimming, jogging or cycling. It is worthwhile finding out which pursuits are attractive to older persons, and encouraging the development of these activities.

4.7.4   Cost

Group exercise has traditionally been thought more successful than an individual programme, both in arousing interest and maintaining motivation (Shephard 1987). However many older people cannot afford to join a fitness class or club, nor to purchase essential equipment such as training shoes. The Canadian Fitness Survey (Shephard 1986) found that cost was an important factor in popularising exercise, the cheaper alternatives such as walking and gardening were preferable, and had a lower dropout rate. Clinical research indicates that vigorous weight-bearing activities, such as brisk walking, are the safest, cheapest, easiest and most beneficial forms of exercise (Edwards and Larson 1992).

4.8   What are the customary activity levels of the third age and are they sufficient to maintain fitness?

Despite the fact that older people have an increased awareness of the importance of being physically fit (National Fitness Survey 1992), only limited numbers participate in exercise appropriate to the maintenance of functional independence; 34% in those aged 55-64 and 23% at 65-74. Even fewer undertake enough exercise to protect against heart disease. Dallosso and colleagues (1988), in a study of community dwelling people in Nottingham, found that only 47% of those 65-74 participated in leisure activities such as swimming and cycling, with time averaging only 2.2 hours/week. The total time spent walking averaged 55 minutes/day and only 29% had walked for more than an hour that day.

The National Fitness Survey (1992) has provided the first comprehensive report concerning the fitness and activity levels of the UK population. In those aged 65-74, 30% of men and 56% of women had Quadriceps strength below that required to stand up from a chair unaided. Of those 55-64, 30% of men and 51% of women were not fit enough to sustain continuous normal paced walking; rising to 45% and 79% respectively for those aged 65-74. These figures were in stark contrast to the self assessment of fitness, of men and women aged 55-74 23% and 26% respectively thought themselves very fit and 56% and 60% fairly fit. However, though most women aged 55-74 reported themselves to be very or fairly fit, yet nearly all women in this age band would find it extremely difficult to walk up a hill with a 5% gradient at 3mph. On a positive note, the percentage of people likely to experience difficulties with simple tasks of everyday life was consistently smaller in those subjects who exercised.

4.9   Why do some people in the third age have low exercise participation?

The National Fitness Survey found that lower educational levels, being female and of older age were associated with poor exercise participation. Gray (1987) discusses several philosophical and cultural factors which may discourage older people from participating in exercise. "It's just my age; it's God's will; I don't want to wear out my body; there's no point in trying" are typical remarks. They reflect the cultural and religious beliefs held by much of the population of Britain, who regard retirement as a period of well deserved rest, and everyday life becoming a struggle as an irreversible consequence of ageing (Gray 1987).

Edwards and Larson (1992) suggest that many people do not know what constitutes "healthful" regular exercise i.e. the kind of exercise that induces a conditioning effect. The National Fitness Survey found that other factors which prevented participation in exercise were injuries or disabilities, "not being the sporty type", medical concerns, wishing to relax in spare time, and a lack of time. Others may include a unawareness of community opportunity and transportation problems (Edwards and Larson 1992). Shephard (1987) suggests that the provision of cheap, adequate and suitable facilities and personnel are of great importance.

4.10   The future

Clearly, it is essential that people regard healthy ageing as a realistic and achievable goal, and appreciate the importance of exercise, and how much and what type of exercise is appropriate. A greater understanding of the reasons why people do not exercise is needed so that intervention can be targeted effectively. It is essential to ensure that exercise is a positive and enjoyable experience. This will require the coordinated action of government bodies, urban planners, leisure facility managers, health professionals, voluntary bodies and numerous others.

Gray (1987) suggests that, because of the growing public interest in leisure pursuits, future cohorts will have more positive attitudes towards exercise and health professionals will promote exercise more vigorously than to date. However, there is no room for complacency and steps must be taken to ensure that this happens.

5   THE SPECIAL SENSES

5.1   Vision

Structural changes that occur to the eye with advancing age include the diminishing ability of ciliary muscles to control the thickness of the lens and therefore to focus it, the diminishing size of the pupil decreasing the amount of light that can enter the eye, the thickening and yellowing of the lens reducing accommodative power and transmission of light entering the eye and the loss of cells from the retina and optic pathway reducing acuity and appreciation of contrast (Weale 1989, Verrillo and Verrillo 1985).

5.1.1   Presbyopia

As a result of age-associated changes in the lens and ciliary muscles, there is a universal loss of accommodation (the power to focus object at different distances) with increasing age. This gives presbyopia or long-sightedness, and begins to affect vision from 15 years onwards, though corrective lenses are not usually required until the middle to late 40s. There is usually a total loss of accommodation by 60 (Verrillo and Verrillo 1985).

5.1.2   Visual Acuity

Static visual acuity is the ability to resolve fine spatial detail and declines from around 45 years of age (Fozard 1990). Mostly it is due to decreased retinal illumination resulting from structural changes affecting light transmission. Thus, increasing luminance and contrast can easily compensate for this deficit. Dynamic visual acuity, the acuity for moving objects, declines more rapidly, however, and is poorly predicted by static visual acuity, particularly when the speed of the moving object is high. This suggests that changes in central processing may be responsible.

5.1.3   Declines in other aspects of vision

The visual field, the extent of sight when fixating forward, is maintained until the age of 35 years and declines slightly between the ages of 40 and 50 and thereafter at a progressively faster rate (Burg 1968). Also, when illumination is low the visual system is able to increase its sensitivity (dark adaptation), usually maximally by 30 minutes. The extent but not the rate of dark adaptation decreases with advancing age (Fozard 1990, Verrillo and Verrillo 1985). In addition there is a progressive decrease in sensitivity to colours, starting around 20 years of age, with deficits becoming most marked at around the age of 70 (Verrillo and Verrillo 1985). Finally, there is an increased sensitivity to glare with advancing age (Kline and Schieber 1985), and older people may take longer to recover from glare (Burg 1967).

5.2   Eye disease

Although visual changes occur as part of a universal physiological aging process, advanced age also leads to increased prevalence of various eye diseases which can impair vision. The four most serious are glaucoma, cataracts, diabetic retinopathy and macular degeneration.

The most comprehensive study of prevalence of these four diseases comes from USA (Leibowitz and colleagues 1980) though there has been a smaller recent British study of those over 65 (Wormald and colleagues 1992). The USA findings for the four major diseases are shown in table 5.1. This study also showed that these four diseases accounted for 42% of poor vision (best eye 20/200 vision or worse) in those aged 52-64, 54% in those 65-74 and 86% over 75. Prevalence of poor vision of this degree was 2.7% aged 52-64, 5.5% aged 65-74 and 14.6% over 75.

Table 5.1

Percentage prevalence of the four main eye diseases in the Framingham Eye Study.

age	cataract	glaucoma	diabetic retinopathy	senile macular degeneration
males				
52-64	3.5	1.5	2.2	0.8
65-74	11.3	3.5	2.9	4.3
75+	33.8	4.4	4.4	16.9
females				
52-64	3.6	0.9	1.4	1.4
65-74	14.2	1.6	2.4	7.9
75+	46.6	3.0	5.9	21.6

(*Source:* Leibowitz and colleagues 1980)

Prevention and treatment of these diseases are thus of great importance. Whilst prevention of cataract is not possible at present, there is effective treatment with particularly good results from lens replacement surgery. Glaucoma can be detected by screening before vision is affected; yields are small but effective treatment is possible. Diabetic retinopathy complicates insulin-dependent diabetes and is less likely where there is high quality control of the disease. Once retinopathy develops, some benefit may be gained from laser therapy. Senile macular degeneration cannot be prevented or treated effectively at the present time. Eye examinations carried out as a part of a visit to an optician are a way in which these important eye pathologies are often first recognised. It is therefore a matter of concern that rates of such examinations should not fall now that they are no longer free under NHS arrangements.

5.3 Hearing impairment

The prevalence of hearing impairment may be estimated from self-reporting or audiometric assessment, loss in the better ear of 25dBHL (decibels hearing loss) providing a "threshold of impairment" with similar prevalence rates to self-reporting, (Haggard and colleagues 1981). However audiometric rates often exceed self-reporting in older subjects, perhaps because of denial or low expectations. In the UK approximately one third of those 61-70 and 60% of those 71-80 have 25dBHL hearing impairment (Davis 1989; Table 5.2). Two million people over 60 suffer from hearing impairment (OPCS 1988). Deterioration in hearing is highly dependent on age rather than initial hearing level. Over 55 loss is 8.6dB/decade, as against 2.5dB under 55 (Davis and colleagues 1991). Annual incidence rates for 25dBHL were estimated as 1.8% at age 55. Table 5.3 shows forecasts for England and Wales of the numbers of deaf (Davis 1991). By 2016 there will be 20% more deaf people than in 1988, most of the increase being among those aged over 60. The increase may be even greater given high noise exposures of many younger people, noise being a risk factor for subsequent hearing loss.

Table 5.2

Percentage prevalence of self-reported and measured hearing impairment.

Age	self reported	›25dBHL	›45dBHL	›65dBHL
17-30	14.1	1.8	0.2	0.0
31-40	20.0	2.8	1.1	0.7
41-50	26.5	8.2	1.7	0.3
51-60	31.2	18.9	4.0	0.9
61-70	35.2	36.8	7.4	2.3
71-80	43.9	60.2	17.6	4.0

(*Source:* Davis 1989)

5.3.1 Provision and Uptake of Hearing Aids

Hearing aids demonstrably benefit hearing impairment (Davis and colleagues 1992, Mulrow and colleagues 1990) yet only around 20-30% of those with hearing impairment thought to justify an aid have one (Herbst and colleagues 1991). The problem is partly poor provision of aids, particularly for older age groups (Davis 1991, Davis and colleagues 1992) perhaps reflecting negative public attitudes to the deaf. Yet projected increase in numbers calls for a 1-2% per annum increase in resources merely to maintain current inadequate provision (Davis 1991). Poor uptake of hearing aids, perhaps a greater problem than poor provision, reflects the stigma attached to hearing aids. Thus making hearing aids less cumbersome and obtrusive may help uptake. Furthermore, gradual hearing loss is often considered "normal" by the aging individual and, too often, by health professionals. Such lowered expectations may be compounded by ignorance of

Table 5.3

Estimated numbers (thousands) of hearing impaired people in England and Wales.

	>25dBHL			>45dBHL			>65dBHL		
	18-60	61-80	80+	18-60	61-80	80+	18-60	61-80	80+
Female									
1991	812	1952	1224	162	552	612	43	152	161
2001	895	1875	1367	182	534	684	51	147	180
2011	926	1994	1413	186	548	706	54	154	186
2016	950	2114	1377	189	586	689	54	164	182
Male									
1991	1116	2089	374	263	466	206	80	114	55
2001	1276	2116	462	304	473	255	91	115	68
2011	1325	2359	538	305	524	297	83	129	79
2016	1389	2489	549	321	554	302	85	136	80

(*Source:* Davis 1991)

services available and by lengthy delays (RNID 1988). The RNID (1988) made proposals for improvements which have not been implemented, although there is now a growing trend towards direct referral from General Practitioners to a hearing aid clinic, eliminating the necessity to see an ENT specialist and its inevitable delay. A Department of Health evaluation comparing traditional and direct referral schemes is in progress and results are due in late 1992.

5.3.2   Use of hearing aids

Even when a hearing aid is available it may not be used. Thomas and Herbst (1981) reported that 17 of individuals rarely or never used their NHS hearing aid. Only 38% said they always wore it. Brooks (1985) found with 40dBHL or less only 14% used the aid more than 8 hours a day rising to 40% for 60dBHL. Low usage may occur for several reasons. Hearing aids are still unable to discriminate successfully between speech and background noise; they cannot restore hearing to the same level of perfection as, say, spectacles can for sight. Some individuals may have difficulties with insertion of the ear piece. Alternatively, there may be an unrealistic belief that the hearing loss does not warrant the use of an aid (Brooks 1985).

5.3.3   Screening for Hearing Loss

Present services rely on individuals seeking help for themselves and many present only late, Stephens and colleagues (1990) finding 15 years of symptoms and average age of 70 at first presentation. This suggests a need for a screening programme and, given the dramatic increase in hearing impairment in the third age, it would be an appropriate time for screening. Efficacy has been demonstrated; uptake of aids rose from 3% to 9% in one study (Davis and colleagues 1992) from 7% to 24% in another and from 8% to 22% in a third (Stephens and colleagues 1990). Simple screening procedures suffice, Stephens and colleagues (1990) finding that postal questionnaires with two postings identified 96% of those who subsequently accepted hearing aids. Screening would introduce hearing aids at an earlier age when greater use is made of them and with fewer handling problems (Brooks 1985, Parving and Philip 1991). Greater use of hearing aids by younger people might help to reduce their stigma. Introduction of a screening programme at retirement age (55-65) has much to commend it and need not be expensive (Davis and colleagues 1992). Screening could minimise years of disability and reduce the numbers of frail elderly, whose deafness would otherwise cause dependence. The relative benefits and costs of nationwide screening need to be properly evaluated, therefore.

5.3.4   Secondary Problems Associated with Hearing Loss

Acquired hearing impairment has a profound negative effect on social, emotional and behavioural function and is strongly associated with depression and social and emotional isolation (Herbst and Humphrey 1980, Thomas and Herbst 1980). Even a mild hearing impairment may interfere with cognitive capabilities by placing extra demand on the information processing capacity of the brain through having to extract sensory information under conditions of adversity so that ability to recognise the spoken word and to remember what is said may be compromised (Rabbitt 1991b). Increased age contributes to this effect but high IQ may protect. Some of the cognitive deficits noticed with advanced years (such as difficulties with remembering) may thus be due to hearing impairment and be rectifiable.

6 DISEASES MAKING MAJOR CONTRIBUTIONS TO MORTALITY

6.1 Ischaemic Heart Disease

Ischaemic heart disease (IHD) is one of the major causes of death and of morbidity in the third age in developed countries. In the UK some 300,000 individuals suffer an acute myocardial infarction each year (Royal College of Physicians 1992) and some 30% of all male deaths and 22% of female deaths are attributable to IHD (Marmot and Mann 1987). In England and Wales IHD is the commonest cause of death in men in all age groups beyond 35 and second only to cancer in women. It is estimated to account for almost half of all life years lost by death before 65 in men whilst circulatory disease, to which IHD is the major contributor, accounts for a quarter of days of certified incapacity in men (Royal College of Physicians 1992).

6.1.1 Differences in IHD rates

The whole of UK has high rates for IHD, its frequency being highest in Scotland, then N Ireland, then Wales and lowest in England (table 6.1). However these differences are less striking than the differences between overall UK rates and those of other developed countries which are generally lower, strikingly so in some instances such as Japan (figure 6.1). Not only are there considerable differences between rates for IHD in different countries but rates have shown considerable changes with time. Encouragingly, rates have fallen appreciably in some countries in recent years, for example in USA, Canada and Australia. The position in the UK has lagged behind these changes but there are strong reasons for optimism that we are now entering a similar phase of improvement. This will be examined in more detail later.

Table 6.1

Mortality rates per 10,000 population for ischaemic heart disease.

country	males 45-54	males 55-64	males 65-74	females 45-54	females 55-64	females 65-74
England	16.3	53.7	131.1	2.9	16.9	59.2
Wales	17.1	61.0	153.9	3.7	18.8	68.2
N Ireland	18.4	69.3	179.2	4.1	23.1	77.5
Scotland	21.1	74.6	171.7	5.4	25.3	85.9

(*Source:* OPCS Mortality Series DH1)

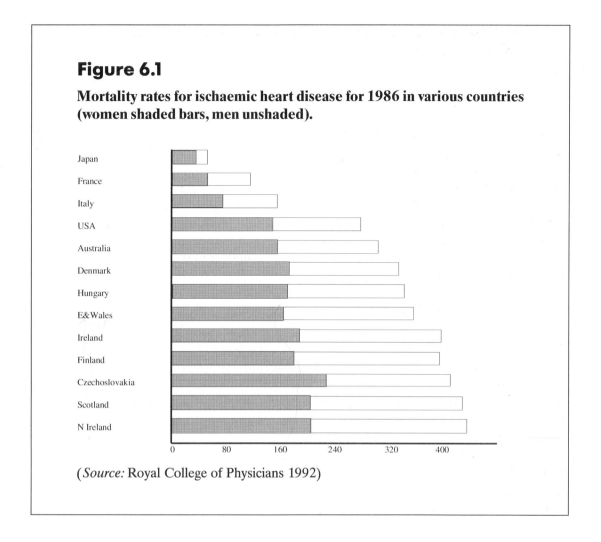

Figure 6.1

Mortality rates for ischaemic heart disease for 1986 in various countries (women shaded bars, men unshaded).

(*Source:* Royal College of Physicians 1992)

6.2 Risk factors for IHD

These findings of international and temporal changes in IHD rates support the view that environmental factors play a strong part in the development of IHD. Detailed epidemiological studies of IHD have allowed some of these risk factors to be identified (reviewed by Marmot and Mann 1987) and the important findings for known risk factors which can be modified will be summarised here.

6.2.1 Smoking

Smoking is a major risk factor for IHD. This was powerfully demonstrated by the classic studies of Doll and Peto (1976) and Doll and colleagues (1980) and confirmed by many others. Risk is related to the number of cigarettes smoked and the relative risk of IHD in smokers compared with non-smokers is greatest at younger ages. Doll and Peto (1976) found the relative risk for death from IHD in male doctors smoking 25 or more cigarettes a day as compared with their non-smoking counterparts to be 15 for those under 45, 2.2 for those aged 45-54, 1.6 for those 55-64 and 1.5 for those 65-74. Because IHD is so common in the third age in the UK, any elevation of relative risk, such as that associated with smoking, will adversely affect large numbers of people. Smoking appears to be particularly dangerous when serum cholesterol is high for in countries such as Japan, where population cholesterol levels are low, smoking appears not to be a risk factor. Relative risk of IHD falls over the years after cessation of smoking (Doll and Peto 1976).

6.2.2   Blood Pressure

In studies from many countries elevated blood pressure is consistently associated with raised IHD risk (see Marmot and Mann 1987). There does not appear to be a threshold level for the effect; risk appears to be rise with blood pressure across the whole range (MacMahon and colleagues 1990). Again the risks associated with blood pressure appear to be influenced by levels of cholesterol, seeming to have little effect on IHD risk in Japan, for example, where levels are low.

6.2.3   Lipids

IHD is uncommon in communities where serum cholesterol levels are low even when risk factors such as smoking or high blood pressure are present. Positive correlations between individuals' serum cholesterol values and subsequent IHD mortality have been shown by many studies and more recent work where fractionation of serum lipids has been performed show that the low density lipoprotein fraction (LDL) is associated with elevated IHD risk whereas high density lipoprotein (HDL) is protective. HDL and LDL levels are influenced by dietary fat intakes. The 'typical western diet' of countries such as the UK which is high in saturated fat and low in polyunsaturated fat is associated with high IHD rates and high cholesterol and LDL values. Conversely, countries with high polyunsaturate/saturate ratios in the national diet have low IHD rates and low cholesterol values.

6.2.4   Coagulation Factors

Blood levels of the clotting factors fibrinogen and Factor VII have been shown to be predictive of IHD levels, high levels being deleterious (Meade and colleagues 1980)

6.2.5   Physical Exercise

Physical exercise has been shown to have a protective effect against IHD. Moderate exercise levels appear adequate to give full protection; indeed an increased risk during vigorous exercise may offset longer term benefits (Shaper and Wannamethee 1991).

6.2.6   Early Life Experience and Socioeconomic Factors

There is an apparent paradox in that, although the rise in IHD in UK this century has been associated with increasing prosperity, mortality rates are now highest in the least affluent. The rates decrease with higher social class and current trends show rates to be falling in upper social classes but to be stationary or rising in the lower ones, contributing to an increasing social class differential in overall mortality (Marmot and McDowall 1986). These differences can partly be accounted for by the effects of smoking.

Barker and Osmond (1986) showed that the rates of IHD in the 212 local authority areas in England and Wales correlated with infant mortality rates 50 years earlier. This suggested that poor nutrition in early life might be an important risk factor for IHD. They have explored this hypothesis in a series of further studies which have been recently reviewed (Barker and Martyn 1992). In a follow-up study of Hertfordshire men born 1911-30 they showed that men with the lowest weights at birth and one year had the highest death rates for IHD though these weights were independent of social class in the men who died (Barker and colleagues 1989).

The group has looked for possible mechanisms for such effects. They have found that blood pressure in later life is correlated with measures of foetal growth, namely birth weight, ponderal index at birth and the ratio of head circumference to length at birth (Law and colleagues 1991). They have been able to correlate the serum risk factors, cholesterol, fibrinogen and Factor VII with measures of early growth and nutrition (Fall and colleagues 1992, Barker and colleagues 1992) and also glucose tolerance, diabetes being a known risk factor for IHD (Hales and colleagues 1991). These risk factor effects appeared to be independent of social class and to remain after allowance for other factors such as smoking. The group's interpretation is that the relation between measures of growth in early life and adult risk of IHD is due to long term effects on physiology and metabolism from adverse circumstances at specific critical periods of development (Barker and Martyn 1992). This programming hypothesis has provoked challenges but is now supported by an impressive weight of evidence (Robinson 1992).

6.3   Trends in IHD mortality rates in the UK

This country has seen major changes in IHD mortality rates during this century. Age specific mortality rates rose progressively up to the 1970s but appear to have peaked and to be now falling: figure 6.2 shows the findings for men aged 55-64 as a typical example. Though all age groups show similar changes, there appears to be a definite cohort effect with improvements in mortality occurring earliest in later cohorts (Osmond and Barker 1991).

6.3.1   Reasons for changes in mortality rates

The improvements in UK can be related to changes in cigarette smoking, the differences between social classes being largely explained by differences in smoking, higher groups having reduced their smoking far more than the lower ones. However this is unlikely to be the sole explanation. The findings of the Barker group also seem important, particularly if one accepts their further suggestion that the combination of poor nutrition in childhood coupled with an affluent nutritional pattern in middle life is particularly deleterious. This would fit with the observed changes where IHD appeared first as a disease of the higher social classes but subsequently changed to one of lower social classes and that later cohorts have shown the most striking decreases in IHD mortality. Specific medical interventions, including management of risk factors and treatment of acute heart attacks, have affected only a minority of people and are not likely to have had much impact so far on total population rates.

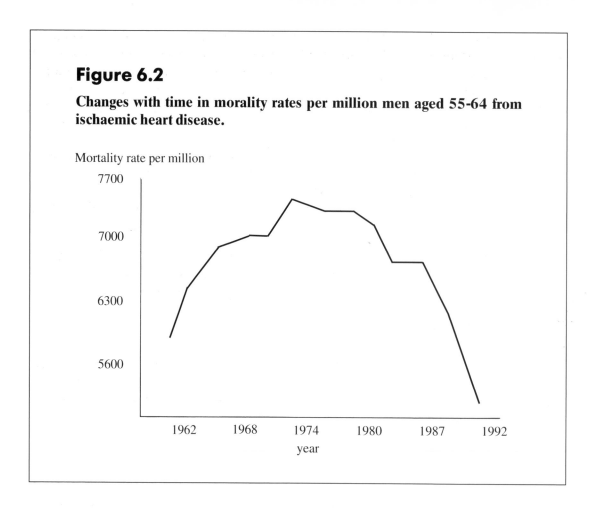

Figure 6.2

Changes with time in morality rates per million men aged 55-64 from ischaemic heart disease.

Mortality rate per million

year

6.4   Possibilities for prevention

Given that a number of risk factors for IHD have been clearly recognised and are potentially reversible, for example smoking, high cholesterol levels, high blood pressure and lack of exercise, the scope for prevention seems clear. However, experience to date has been disappointing where community based programmes of risk factor intervention have been undertaken (see reviews by Marmot and Mann 1987, Royal College of Physicians 1992 and Oliver 1992).

A number of reasons have been offered for the failure of most of these planned intervention trials to demonstrate benefits despite the strong circumstantial evidence, for example that of Doll and Peto (1976) as to the benefits of cessation of smoking. Most trials were in countries where participants had considerable knowledge about risk factors so that behaviour changed in both intervention and control groups, considerably weakening power of trials. Where drugs were used to treat high blood pressure or high lipids, these may have increased non-cardiac deaths so that, whilst there may have been a reduction of cardiac deaths, the fall in total deaths was not statistically significant. There is recent concern over some studies that have suggested a specific increase in deaths from violence and suicide in the actively treated groups. A further consideration is that interventions may not have been focused on groups at sufficiently high risk. Furthermore, intervention in middle age may be too late to be really effective. Far better results might occur if behaviours such as smoking and inadequate exercise could be avoided from youth; risk factors best predict IHD in the youngest age groups and risk factor modification may only be truly effective before IHD has developed. Finally, interventions may have been insufficiently stringent as trial evidence does suggest that rigorous intervention, specifically to reduce smoking and high cholesterol values by diet, may be effective (Oliver 1992).

The present status of interventional policies is thus far from clear but it would seem prudent to promote measures to reduce smoking, avoid low exercise levels and eat diets with higher polyunsaturate/saturate fat levels on a whole community basis. Such a strategy, starting at a young age and continuing, may have lasting impact throughout adult life.

Given the findings of the Barker group on programming in foetal and infant life, the avoidance by mothers of smoking and alcohol and the promotion of good nutrition during pregnancy might have a considerable impact on future rates of IHD.

6.4.1   Familial IHD

Young victims of IHD commonly have a family history of IHD. In a about a fifth of cases there are identifiable genetic defects leading to hypercholesterolaemia. Overall some 1% of the population has a genetic predisposition to premature IHD and correction of environmental risk factors would seem to be particularly important in such individuals (Royal College of Physicians 1992).

6.4.2   Oestrogens and IHD

Premenopausal women have far lower levels of IHD than men but this protection is lost after the menopause and values climb towards those of men. Hormone replacement therapy thus may have some potential as a preventive measure in postmenopausal women but would need to be continued long term. It is unlikely that this could be justified for IHD alone, the best case for long term hormone replacement therapy being in the prevention of osteoporosis and fractures. The protection against IHD would however be a useful secondary benefit.

6.4.3   Aspirin in the prevention of IHD

Aspirin in small daily dosage has effects on clotting factors and has been shown to be capable of reducing IHD mortality, by 44% in the American Physicians' Health Study (Steering Committee 1989). However, protection was bought at the expense of complications that necessitate restricting this preventive measure to people at particularly high risk of IHD.

6.5   Treatment of established IHD

IHD can be thought of as having two phases. Firstly vessels of the heart are compromised by deposition of fatty atheromatous deposits in their walls at which stage the disease is usually asymptomatic. Secondly these lesions may rupture and thrombosis be superimposed so that there is acute deterioration in blood supply to the heart and illness in the form of unstable angina, myocardial infarction and acute cardiac death. For many years medical treatment of such acute events has relied on anticoagulant drugs (aiming to counteract further thrombosis) but recent years have seen the introduction of effective thrombolytic therapy (aiming to reverse thrombosis).

Thrombolytic therapy has been recently reviewed by Wilcox (1991). The combination of aspirin with streptokinase, anistreplase or alteplase can reduce mortality after myocardial infarction by 25-40% and this gain in early survival appears to be maintained for at least a year. This would not appear to be at the cost of survival in a more functionally disabled state and so appears to be a real improvement. However, though valuable in terms of those who become victims of IHD, the impact of this treatment advance on mortality of the whole community from IHD is likely to be marginal as would appear to have been the case for other treatment advances in the past, for example the establishment of specialist coronary care units. In policy terms we would be wise to concentrate on prevention if we wish to achieve the greatest benefits from our efforts.

6.6   Future Trends for IHD

As illustrated in figure 6.2, rates for IHD in the third age are now in decline in UK. Furthermore, if we are to judge from experience in countries such as the USA and Australia, the UK still has a long way to go in terms of further improvements. Osmond and Barker (1991) have made a detailed examination of present trends and cohort effects and have based forecasts extending to 2007 for all of England and Wales and regions. They predict large falls in rates for IHD, particularly below the age of 65. Their predicted falls in IHD mortality for the 20 years 1983-1987 to 2003-2007 for the age groups 50-54, 55-59, 60-64, 65-69 and 70-74 are respectively to 58%, 59%, 65%, 76% and 82% for men and 56%, 61%, 63%, 82% and 94% for women.

They do however caution that there is likely to be an increase in the present north/south divide so that the northern experience becomes even more unfavourable in comparison with that of the south. They suggest that preventive measures might thus be given particular priority in the north. This is also an important priority for Northern Ireland and Scotland which have high rates compared with England now and whose relative performance will lag further behind in the future if there is no modification of present trends.

6.7   Stroke

Stroke is one of most important cause of death and disability in the third age. Mortality rates from stroke have been falling in the USA since 1900, in Australia from 1950 and in New Zealand since the late 1970s. In England and Wales, also, mortality rates for stroke have been falling (Grimley Evans, 1986). Rates among men aged 45 to 84 have been falling at a rate of approximately 2 to 3% per annum since the early 1950s. At ages 25 to 44 rates were constant until the late 1960s and have been falling since then. The picture is essentially similar in women except that there is more suggestion of declining rates prior to 1950 in those 45-64 whilst under 45 there is little of decline except in the most recent years. In the USA and New Zealand, but not in Britain, there was a biphasic decline in stroke mortality rates with a steady background decline followed by a more rapid decline of rather abrupt onset in the 1970s. This rapid recent decline has been attributed   to community programmes for the control of hypertension but the earlier decline suggests that dietary and lifestyle risk factors for hypertension or stroke may have been undergoing change before hypertension detection and treatment programmes became widespread. Possibilities include a decline in nephritis as a cause of hypertension (Reid and Grimley Evans 1970) or, as Joossens (1973) suggests, that a secular decline in dietary sodium has reduced the prevalence of hypertension. Barker and colleagues (1989) have linked regional mortality rates for stroke to maternal and perinatal mortality rates half a century earlier. They suggest that one of the determinants of stroke lies in the mechanisms of fetal adaptation to maternal malnutrition. This programming may lead to permanent metabolic consequences through its effect on development of tissues that do not change after birth. Thus stroke incidence rates may have been falling because of improvements in maternal nutrition over the earlier years of this century.

On the other hand, the decline in mortality rates from stroke might not be due to changes in incidence at all. Changes in death certification practice or improved treatment leading to a fall in case-fatality might be responsible. Rochester NY offers the only long-term dataset linking incidence to mortality data over a prolonged period (1949 to 1984). The data show a decline in 30-day fatality from 33% in 1945-9 to 20% in 1975-9. The Rochester data also, however, show a decline in incidence rates of stroke. Standardised annual incidence rates of stroke per 100,000 fell from 209 for men and 155 for women to 124 and 68 respectively over the study period (Broderick and colleagues 1989). The decline in incidence in Rochester ceased in the late 1970s and rates actually began to rise after 1980. The authors attribute this rise to the increased use of Computerised Tomographic scanning and the consequent increased detection of minor forms of cerebrovascular disease. Their interpretation of the data is that the stabilisation of stroke incidence had antedated this effect of increased detection.

6.7.1 Stroke incidence rates in the United Kingdom

Direct estimates of stroke incidence in the UK are sparse. The Oxfordshire Stroke Registration Project monitored cases of possible stroke arising within a group of co-operating general practices 1981-1984 (Bamford and colleagues 1990). Incidence rates in the Newcastle Age Research Project (Grimley Evans 1987) relating to ages 65 and over were some 40 higher in men and 60 higher in women than in the Oxfordshire study (Figure 6.3) but related to a region of England with higher mortality rates from stroke (and most other causes of death) and were collected some five years earlier.

Bonita (1992) has estimated that the cumulative risk of stroke for a person of 45 is 3% in both sexes by the age of 65 and 10% for men and 6% for women by the age of 75. In looking to the future in the UK it seems reasonable to expect that the decline in stroke mortality does indicate in part an underlying decline in incidence. We may expect this decline to continue at least while the detection and treatment of hypertension become more effectively deployed in the general population. If the Rochester experience is a foreshadowing of our own, stroke incidence is likely to stabilise during the 1990s.

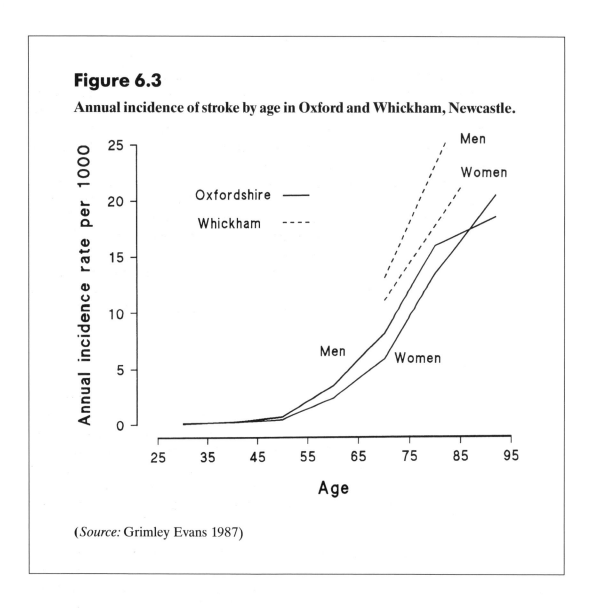

Figure 6.3

Annual incidence of stroke by age in Oxford and Whickham, Newcastle.

(*Source:* Grimley Evans 1987)

6.7.2 Blood pressure and stroke

Whisnant (1984) has suggested that high blood pressure may account for as many as 70 of strokes. Control of blood pressure has been shown to reduce the risk of stroke in middle aged and elderly subjects but the cost-benefit ratio of hypertension detection and treatment remains rather undefined for the milder forms of 'hypertension'. In middle age, where incidence rates of stroke are low, many people will have to receive treatment for several years in order to prevent one stroke though in later life, where incidence rates are higher, the cost-benefit ratio might be more favourable. Blood pressure treatment also carries a burden of side effects that complicate management and reduce compliance. It is not clear that the quality of supervision of blood pressure treatment will be as good in the context of British primary care as it was in the relevant controlled trials.

6.7.3 Heart disease and stroke

There is a clear epidemiological association between the presence of heart disease, and specifically of coronary heart disease, and stroke. The relationship is causal in the acute situation where a recent myocardial infarct leads to mural thrombus and cerebral embolism. Rheumatic valve disease is also a source of cerebral embolism in some situations but is no longer a major cause of stroke in the UK. It is to be hoped that the fall in coronary heart disease incidence in UK, similar to that seen earlier in the USA, will be associated with a decline in stroke risk. The increasing use of aspirin prophylaxis in patients following myocardial infarction may also be expected to have modest beneficial effect on stroke incidence reducing the risk of thromboembolic stroke though with some increase in cerebral haemorrhage. In healthy population groups not at enhanced risk of thromboembolic stroke aspirin may have a net harmful effect by producing more cerebral haemorrhages than the thromboembolic strokes it prevents. In those groups who through previous episodes of coronary heart disease or transient ischaemic attacks are at demonstrably above average risk of thromboembolic stroke, aspirin produces net benefit.

6.7.4 Atrial fibrillation and stroke

Though young adults do not appear to have an increased risk, in middle age and beyond the relative risk of stroke in people with atrial fibrillation is of the order of 3 to 5 and approximately 15% of strokes occur in subjects with fibrillation (Wolf, Abbott and Kannel 1987). The prevalence of atrial fibrillation in British people aged 65 and over is of the order of 5% (Grimley Evans 1985). Data from USA suggest that over the age range 55-74 the annual incidence increases from around 1 to 10 per thousand in men and from 0.5 to 6 per thousand in women (Wolf, Abbott and Kannel 1987) and the risk of stroke appears to be particularly high at the time of onset of atrial fibrillation.

Recent large randomised controlled trials indicate that anticoagulant therapy can reduce the risk of stroke in atrial fibrillation by approximately 30-40% (The Stroke Prevention in Atrial Fibrillation Investigators 1991) and that the degree of anticoagulation required is only moderate (The Boston Area Anticoagulation Trial for Atrial Fibrillation Investigators 1990) so that the incidence of important side-effects is low. However, follow-up has been short so far and the risk/benefit ratio may change with increased duration as the cumulative incidence of haemorrhagic side effects increases.

6.7.5 Diet and stroke

In contrast with coronary heart disease, stroke is not powerfully related to blood lipids, particularly in later life. There is growing evidence that blood pressure, the most powerful risk factor for stroke, can be influenced by the dietary intake of sodium and potassium. Wald, Frost and Law (1991) have reviewed the data on the subject and conclude that diets high in sodium and low in potassium will on a population basis lead to higher blood pressures, effects being most pronounced in later life. There seem good grounds for a reduction in the average levels of salt consumption in the population as recommended by the World Health Organisation and endorsed by the Department of Health.

6.7.6   Smoking and stroke

Though relative risks of stroke associated with smoking decline with age, British data (Shaper and colleagues 1991) indicate that smoking is an important modifiable risk factor for stroke in middle life. Smoking is associated with increase in blood viscosity which favours stroke and has effects on platelet function and fibrinogen which favour thrombosis. Smoking may also be linked indirectly with stroke through its stronger association with coronary heart disease which is a powerful risk factor for stroke. However, there are no data from randomised controlled trials that could provide an adequate basis for estimating the magnitude of the benefit of smoking control on stroke risk.

6.7.7   Alcohol and stroke

The relationship between alcohol consumption and stroke is controversial. Alcohol intake is related to blood pressure, and men in alcohol-related occupations show generally high Standardised Mortality Rates for stroke though the association might be due to the confounding effect of smoking. In addition to the chronic association of alcohol with stroke, there is also the issue of an acute effect of 'binge' drinking and stroke. This was originally postulated in studies from Finland (Hillbom and Kaste 1981) drawing attention to the high incidence of stroke in young men on the traditional drinking days (Friday and Saturday) of Finnish urban society. Studies elsewhere have provided little support for the concept, and it has not been demonstrated in women or older men, but this may reflect a lower frequency of binge drinking.

6.7.8   Stroke, the future

As indicated earlier, survival following stroke has probably improved since the 1950s but mostly through improved supportive therapy and non-specific facilitation of spontaneous recovery. While more can be done for stroke victims than commonly is done, a major advance in rehabilitation could only be expected from some means of reconstructing damaged brain tissue. Research into nerve growth factors offers this as a distant hope, but seems unlikely to bear fruit within the present decade. For the foreseeable future, reductions in stroke-associated disability can only be achieved through primary prevention.

It seems likely that a modest reduction in the incidence of stroke contributes to the decline in stroke mortality in the UK. If, as seems likely, the situation in the USA foreshadows what will happen here, this spontaneous decline may be expected to cease during the decade of the 1990s. We may expect that further decline might be achieved by improved detection and treatment of high blood pressure as public and professional awareness increase and a wider range of effective and more acceptable drugs becomes available. Modification of diet to reduce salt intake may produce further falls in average population blood pressures. A reduction in smoking would contribute to a decline in stroke incidence through other mechanisms. A further modest reduction in incidence of the order of 5% might be expected from a programme of detection and anticoagulant treatment of atrial fibrillation. It is not realistic to try to make firm estimates of the effects of all these factors but given that present trends seem to be in a positive direction we can perhaps expect a 20 to 30% reduction in stroke incidence in the third age by the year 2001. In the anticipated absence of major developments in rehabilitative measures during this period the reduction in disability from stroke will be of the same order.

6.8   Malignancies in the third age

There follow brief descriptions of the epidemiology of the malignancies which are numerically the most important as causes of mortality in the third age. Registration rates are given in table 6.2 and have generally risen over the period 1971-1986. Risk factors for individual conditions in the third age are similar to those at other ages.

6.8.1   Lung cancer

Lung cancer accounts for about 26% of all cancers in males and 12% of cancers in females in the third age in Britain. Until the 1920s it was an uncommon disease. By the 1950s the age-standardised mortality rates for lung cancer in Britain in men had increased 20-fold. It is now well recognised that over 90% of all lung cancer in Britain is attributable to tobacco smoking. Incidence rates have been considerably lower in women than men (reflecting past smoking differences). In the last couple of decades, however, the incidence of lung cancer in men has started to decline (as has that in young women) whilst the incidence in older women is increasing, reflecting changing patterns of tobacco consumption. Occupational exposures (e.g. to asbestos and polycyclic hydrocarbons) are also recognised risk factors for a minority of cases of lung cancer.

6.8.2   Large bowel cancer

Cancers of the colon and rectum count for about 11% of all cancers in the third age. International variation in the incidence is marked, being considerably higher in developed countries, perhaps because of the "western" diet, but specific causes are unknown.

6.8.3   Stomach cancer

In Britain stomach cancer accounts for about 5% of all cancers in the third age. There is wide variation in incidence internationally (with particularly high rates in Japan and parts of China). Within Britain its incidence is gradually declining and is higher in the north than south and higher in the west than east. It is considerably more common in lower social classes. Genetic factors play some part in its aetiology and diet is almost certainly important. However, despite a number of clues, there is no firm evidence about the major causes of this cancer.

6.8.4   Bladder cancer

Bladder cancers account for about 5% of all cancers in the third age. The most important known aetiological agent is cigarette smoking. Other chemical exposures (e.g. in the dye and rubber industries) are implicated but their total contribution to overall incidence is fairly small.

6.8.5 Leukaemias and Lymphomas

These conditions account for about 5% of malignancies in Britain in the third age. Ionising radiation is a recognised risk factor for leukaemia but accounts for small numbers of cases. Other recognised causes in a minority of cases include certain chemicals and medicinal agents. However, the cause of the majority of cases is unknown.

6.8.6　Breast cancer

Cancer of the breast accounts for about a quarter of cancers in women in the third age in Britain. There is striking variation in its incidence internationally. In general, it is much more common in the developed countries where it has increased in recent decades. Dietary factors have been implicated but not precisely defined. The lifetime duration of ovarian activity appears important as the disease is more common in women who have an early menarche and a late menopause than in others. An early age of first full-term pregnancy also seems protective against breast cancer later in life. There is conflicting evidence about whether long duration of use of oral contraceptives, particularly prior to the birth of the first child, is a risk factor. Despite various clues about aetiology, for the most part it remains unknown.

6.8.7　Cancers of the Uterus

Cancer of the uterine cervix accounts for 2% of cancers in women in the third age in Britain. Squamous cell carcinoma, the common type, is associated with high sexual activity, particularly number of sexual partners (either of the woman or her partner). Other factors include cigarette smoking and, possibly, the use of oral contraceptives.

Cancer of the endometrium (body of the uterus) accounts for about 4% of all cancers in women in the third age. The risk of the disease is higher in nulliparous women than others but is unrelated to the number of sexual partners. Like cancer of the breast, it is associated with early menarche and late menopause. Exposure to the intake of oestrogens is also a recognised risk factor.

6.8.8　Cancer of the Ovary

Cancer of the ovary accounts for about 5% of cancers in women in the third age. The incidence of the disease is decreased by the use of oral contraceptives. In rare instances ovarian cancer occurs in families and is considered to have a genetic component. Its causes are otherwise unknown.

6.8.9　Cancer of the Prostate

Cancer of the prostate accounts for about 8% of cancers in men in the third age. Its aetiology is unknown.

6.8.10 Cancer of the Pancreas

Cancer of the pancreas accounts for about 3% of cancers in the third age. It is about twice as common in regular cigarette smokers than in non-smokers. Incidence correlates with high standards of living but, otherwise, its aetiology is unknown.

6.8.11 Oesophageal cancer

Cancer of the oesophagus accounts for about 2% of all cancers in the third age. Incidence rates vary considerably internationally and Britain is not a particularly high-risk area. In Britain, risk relates to smoking and alcohol consumption. Incidence fell progressively earlier this century with the decline in alcohol consumption but has increased in recent decades, notably in middle-aged men, with rising consumption.

6.9 Chronic bronchitis

Chronic Bronchitis remains a major contributor to deaths from respiratory diseases which form the third largest category of deaths in those aged 55-64 behind cancers and heart disease and a close fourth in those ages 65-74 behind heart disease, cancers and cerebrovascular disease (OPCS 1991).

Yet mortality rates for chronic bronchitis have shown impressive declines in Britain, for example total deaths in England and Wales falling from a peak level of 30,001 in 1963 to 11,793 in 1984 and to 4,934 in 1990 (Registrar General's Statistical Returns 1962, 1972, OPCS 1991). These dramatic falls in total deaths have greatly benefitted those in the third age, especially men in whom rates have always been far higher than women. Figure 6.4 shows the very dramatic nature of this decline for men aged 55-64, similar changes having taken place for mortality rates for both sexes and in the age groups 45-54 and 65-74.

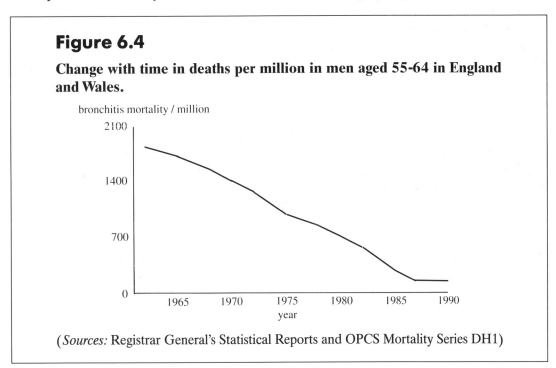

Figure 6.4

Change with time in deaths per million in men aged 55-64 in England and Wales.

(*Sources:* Registrar General's Statistical Reports and OPCS Mortality Series DH1)

It does not seem likely that advances in medical treatment could account for these dramatic changes, rather we should look to the known risk factors for development of the disease; smoking, childhood respiratory tract infections, adequacy of fetal growth and atmospheric pollution.

Chief among these is smoking. The studies of Doll and Peto (1976) and Doll and colleagues (1980) on British doctors found that the relative risks in smokers compared with non-smokers were higher for chronic bronchitis than for other smoking-related diseases. Burrows and colleagues (1988) found virtually no evidence of decline in respiratory function (such as results from chronic bronchitis) in middle aged non-smokers when asthmatics were excluded whereas they found declines in smokers which could be related to pack-years of smoking experience. Declines in population rates for smoking are thus major contributors to falling mortality and morbidity rates for chronic bronchitis but are not the only factor.

The remaining risk factors have also shown improvements which can be presumed to have played their part. A relationship between childhood chest infections and respiratory disease in later life has been shown for 20 year olds by Colley, Douglas and Reid (1973), and has been confirmed in the middle aged by Barker and Osmond (1986). Barker (1991) has also found that low birth weight indicative of poorer maternal nutrition and health and poor fetal growth is associated with higher rates for chronic bronchitis in middle life. Air pollution may not be a particularly strong initiating factor in adult life (Colley, Douglas and Reid 1973, Barker and Osmond 1986) but it may be important as a cause of childhood chest infections. So too may passive smoking experience, children of smoking parents having a greater likelihood of chest infections (Leeder and colleagues 1976).

If population smoking rates continue to fall, we can expect the steep decline in chronic bronchitis to continue. This will have effects on mortality in the third age but the even more striking effects on morbidity in the age group should be borne in mind for sufferers typically have many years of disability before their deaths.

7   IMPORTANT CAUSES OF PHYSICAL DISABILITY

7.1   Osteoarthritis

Rheumatic complaints, arthritis and soft-tissue symptoms rank high among the conditions causing lost days of work and leisure in middle life and beyond. By far the commonest of this group of disorders causing symptoms and disability is osteoarthritis. The majority of people have some degree of osteoarthritis by the age of 65 and more than 80 by the age of 75. However, there is a poor correlation between the signs and the symptoms of osteoarthritis and an even poorer correlation between symptoms and radiological evidence of the condition. For example less than half of the people with radiological evidence of osteoarthritis of the knee complain of pain. One question about osteoarthritis is whether each joint is affected as a separate entity or whether there is a tendency to affect multiple joints. It does appear that some people show a greater propensity for multiple joint involvement than do others, and that some manifestations of osteoarthritis such as Heberden's nodes have a genetic component. Several mechanisms may underlie generalised osteoarthritis. These include metabolically determined crystal deposition in joints, minor abnormalities of collagen or secondary changes in joints slightly damaged by previous episodes of an unrelated polyarthropathy.

While osteoarthritis may affect almost any joint, the joints of the spinal column, the knee and the hip produce the most morbidity. In the third age the last two are the most significant.

7.1.1   Osteoarthritis of the knee

Prevalence of osteoarthritis of the knees increases in both sexes over the age range 55-74. It is symptomatic in a smaller proportion of men than women, perhaps because men are more able than women to adopt social roles that produce fewer symptoms. Broad estimates of the relevance of radiological and symptomatic osteoarthritis of the knee in the third age are set out in table 7.1. These figures give a broad estimate of the proportion of people whose wellbeing is in some degree impaired and an upper limit to the proportions who might be candidates for knee replacement surgery should that reach the satisfactory stage of technical development of hip replacement.

Risk factors for osteoarthritis of the knee

Age is a potent risk factor for osteoarthritis of the knee, perhaps by the progressive accumulation of minor trauma and imperfect repair mechanisms. In the third age women are more frequently affected and typically several joints are involved, neither parity nor early menopause appearing to have an influence.

Obesity and osteoarthritis of the knee

There is a consistent association of osteoarthritis of the knee with obesity. Prospectively, there is a strong link between being overweight in the past and having osteoarthritis of the knee later (Felson and colleagues 1988). Furthermore, women who give a history of weight loss are less likely to have symptomatic osteoarthritis of the knee (Felson and colleagues 1992). Thus, obesity causes symptomatic osteoarthritis and British data on height and weight (Knight 1984) indicate that approximately 9% of men and 14% of women will be at enhanced risk because of obesity.

Table 7.1

Estimated percentage prevalence of radiologically (R) and symptomatically (S) defined osteoarthritis of the knee.

age group	R men	S men	R women	S women
35-44	2.7	0.6	3.4	1.1
45-54	5.6	1.2	8.2	2.7
55-64	10.0	2.2	14.1	4.6
65-74	14.9	3.3	23.4	7.7
75+	20.5	4.5	41.8	13.8

(*Source:* Felson 1988)

Occupation and trauma and osteoarthritis of the knee

The association of osteoarthritis of the knee with previous trauma seems well established. Anderson and Felson (1988) report an analysis of occupational data for people aged 35 to 64 using data from the US Department of Labor Dictionary of Occupations in which the strength required for particular jobs and the use of knee bending were coded. The results suggested that prolonged years in an occupation requiring knee bending may predispose to osteoarthritis of the joint in both sexes. A similar relationship with strength exerted in occupations was only significant in women.

Smoking and arthritis

In USA data (Felson and colleagues 1989) smoking appeared to be negatively associated with radiological osteoarthritis. Though the association was independent of age, sex and body weight, there may have been inadequate adjustment for physical and sporting activity.

Chondrocalcinosis

Linear calcification of articular cartilage due to deposits of calcium pyrophosphate dihydrate increases with age (Felson and colleagues 1989) from 3.2% under 70 to 27.1% over 85. However, though this chondrocalcinosis makes osteoarthritis 50% more likely, the proportion of osteoarthritis possibly attributable to it is only of the order of 4%.

7.1.2 Osteoarthritis of the hip

Osteoarthritis of the hip differs in several ways from that of the knee and several other joints. It affects predominantly men and shows a distinct pattern of geographical variation. For example it is much rarer in Chinese and black populations than in Western Europeans even though there is little difference between races in the prevalence of osteoarthritis of other joints. Felson (1988) quotes pooled prevalence results from a number of surveys for those 55-64 years old. Radiological osteoarthritis of hip of grade 2 or worse occurred in 14% of men and 8% of women but grade 3 or worse in 4% and 2% respectively.

In general osteoarthritis of the hip is much less related to factors such as obesity and repetitive use which are risk factors for osteoarthritis of other joints, particularly the knee. It mainly arises as a secondary response to some deformity of the joint surfaces and the main determinants of the wide variation in prevalence observed between population groups may be developmental irregularities of the hip joint. None of the grosser causes such as congenital dislocation of the hip, Perthes disease and slipped femoral capital epiphysis is common in the UK.

7.1.3 Requirements for hip and knee replacement

Osteoarthritis of knees and hips is an important source of discomfort and functional limitation in later life. Around 5% of people over 55 will have problems with knees and a slightly smaller proportion with hips; disease will tend to be bilateral. There is nothing to suggest significant changes in incidence or prevalence and there appears to be little scope for a preventive approach except through the control of obesity and occupational damage to knee joints.

Frankel and colleagues (1990) have reviewed the data on hip and knee replacement surgery in the UK. They note that rates of hip replacement have reached a plateau but that increasing numbers of operations are for revision. There are also problems arising from the increasing use of hip arthroplasty as an immediate treatment for fractures of the proximal femur, a factor that also makes international comparisons of operation rates difficult to evaluate. They estimate current operation rates for total hip replacement in England at 54 per 100,000/year compared with 108 in France, 84 in Denmark and 116 in Belgium. They conclude that a modest increase in present rates of hip replacement to approximately 70 per 100,000/year would be sufficient for incident cases plus revision procedures, but as there has been no study of incidence of the disease this comfortable conclusion must be regarded as provisional. It is not clear whether rates of operation have stabilised in recent years because of satisfied demand or saturated capacity. Since one operation in eight at present is a revision procedure, it is also possible that rates are stabilising because of more stringent criteria being adopted for the initial replacements as part of clinical cost-utility adjustments.

Rates for knee replacement are rising steeply as operative techniques have improved. As prevalence rates for symptomatic knee and hip osteoarthritis are broadly similar, one might expect the operation rates for the two conditions to converge if, as seems plausible, the incidence rates are also similar. For both procedures a good outcome in terms of pain relief can be expected in 80% of cases. There is at present only limited experience of the problems of revision procedures in total knee replacement and this will need to be one of the factors to be considered in identifying appropriate operation rates.

Available data are inadequate for health service planning. There is a need for studies to reassess the prevalence and incidence of hip and knee osteoarthritis and their associated morbidity, and to identify whether available surgical treatment is actually reaching all the people who could benefit from it.

7.2   Osteoporosis, falls and fractures

In osteoporosis bone tissue is weak but structurally normal and there is, in essence, a reduced amount of bone tissue per volume of anatomical bone. Weakness of bone is only one of the factors determining the risk of fracture from falling; protective factors such as neuromuscular responses to falling and the cushioning effects of subcutaneous fat also seem important. Although osteoporosis may be considered to contribute to the incidence of all fractures in later life, the three common fractures most closely associated with the condition are those of the distal forearm, the vertebrae and the proximal femur.

7.2.1   Distal forearm fractures

Distal forearm fractures are common among adolescents of both sexes but thereafter in men rates remain fairly low and constant throughout life. In women there is a large stepwise increase in risk in middle life followed by a pattern of oscillations due in part to an interaction between osteoporosis and a brief peak in the incidence of falls among women aged 45 to 60 (Winner, Morgan and Grimley Evans 1989).

7.2.2   Vertebral fractures

The impact of vertebral fractures upon quality of life in the third age has been under-estimated. Apart from the usually short-lived pain associated with the acute fracture, the subsequent deformity of the thoracic cage, "Dowager's hump" is seen as one of the disfigurements of ageing and may also impair respiratory function and muscular ability. The most comprehensive prevalence data come from Rochester USA (Melton and colleagues 1989; Table 7.2). Rates include 3% of fractures due to severe trauma; the remainder being spontaneous "osteoporotic" fractures.

7.2.3   Proximal femoral fractures

Proximal femoral fracture (PPF) is a serious fracture carrying considerable mortality and long-term morbidity. Although the most severe effects are seen in the very aged, PFF can precipitate restriction of lifestyle at any age.

At ages up to about 55 proximal femoral fractures (PFF) are more common in men and are usually associated with severe trauma, eg road traffic accidents. Above 55, rates start to rise in women, doubling every seven years over 65. In men there is a similar rate of exponential increase over 65 but the absolute rates lag by around ten years of age behind those of women. Approximately 2% of men and 3% of women in UK will experience a PFF before the age of 75 (Law, Wald and Meade, 1991). Incidence has been increasing in the UK over the last 30 years (Boyce and Vessey 1985) but hospital admission rates in

Table 7.2

Smoothed percentage prevalence and estimated incidence per 1000 per annum of one or more vertebral fractures for white women in Rochester Minnesota.

Age group	% prevalence	incidence
50-54	5.9	5.2
55-59	8.3	7.3
60-64	11.7	10.1
65-69	16.2	13.8
70-74	21.9	18.2
75-79	29.0	23.4
80-84	37.4	28.9
85-89	46.5	34.0

(*Source:* Melton and colleagues 1989)

both sexes may have levelled off since 1979 (Spector, Cooper and Fenton Lewis 1990). The rise may have been due to an increased prevalence of osteoporosis, though there is no direct UK evidence for this, or to environmental and lifestyle changes affecting the frequency and consequences of falls.

7.2.4   Osteoporosis and femoral fractures

Differences in bone density between people with and without PFF are on average small and diminish with age (Law, Wald and Meade 1991). Some authors therefore suggest that osteoporosis is irrelevant to PFF and that preventive measures should focus on the other factors (falls and protective responses). However, osteoporosis is underestimated as a risk factor for PFF at later ages because bone density falls with age to a degree where nearly all women over 80 have bones below the fracture threshold so that fractures will be explained by other factors. Nonetheless, the overall incidence of fractures is determined by the proportion of the population whose bone strength lies below fracture threshold and a means of preventing bone loss in middle age or earlier could be expected to have a major impact on the incidence of PFF in later life.

7.2.5   Falls

There is a considerable literature on the epidemiology of falls and of fallers, mostly in populations of people aged over 65. Some medications, notably hypnotics anti-depressants and sedatives are risk factors. The longer-acting drugs seem particularly hazardous in falls generating fractures. Alcohol does not emerge as an important factor in British populations. Hazards in the home environment such as loose mats and trailing electric leads, though associated with falls, offer little preventive scope (Campbell and colleagues 1990). Perhaps it is more promising to focus on hazards in the public environment. Falls involving steps and stairs are particularly hazardous and Archea (1985) and others have studied the effect of stair design on the risk of falls. Confusing visual cues, and stairs that break a natural rhythm of walking can cause unnecessary problems. There is scope for British architects to become more sensitive to the perceptual and motor limitations of an ageing population.

7.2.6 Risk factors, treatment and prevention of osteoporosis

Alcohol and smoking

Alcoholics have low bone density but moderate alcohol intake is not associated with low bone density. Cigarette smoking is associated with lower bone density in postmenopausal women and in 70-year old men but is not a powerful risk factor for PFF (Law, Wald and Meade 1991). It is however associated with vertebral fractures which occur at a younger age than femoral fractures. Reduction in smoking among women would be expected to produce a significant reduction in fractures in later life.

Genetic factors

Women whose mothers suffered from osteoporosis are more likely to develop the condition. It is not known whether this is due to genetics or to habits of diet and lifestyle. Genetic influences on bone mass seems largely responsible for the lower incidence of osteoporotic fractures in black Americans than in white.

Thiazide Medication

Several studies have demonstrated that thiazide diuretics have a favourable effect on bone density and on the incidence of fractures (Ray and colleagues 1989; LaCroix and colleagues 1990). This effect is of sufficient magnitude (a reduction of a third in the risk of hip fracture in older people) to choose thiazides, where clinically appropriate, as first-line treatment for hypertension in patients in middle age and beyond.

Hormone replacement therapy (HRT)

Bone loss rises during the five to ten years immediately following the menopause. This loss can be retarded by oestrogen therapy and studies suggest reduction in incidence of PFF. However, when HRT is stopped, accelerated bone loss analogous to that seen after an unmodified menopause occurs. The question is whether this loss after stopping HRT means that nothing has been gained or whether the risk of fracture in a woman who took HRT for x years after the menopause will always be that of an untreated woman x years younger with the same age of menopause. A recent review suggests that benefits of HRT for hip fracture diminish with time since stopping HRT (Law, Wald and Meade 1991). However, as time since stopping HRT correlates with age and with steeply rising incidence rates for PFF, there will be diminishing benefit as expressed in relative risk even though the absolute benefit is constant. Furthermore, HRT may not only reduce risk of fractures by affecting bone density; muscle strength improves and the enhanced risk of falls in the perimenopausal period identified by Winner and colleagues (1989) may be oestrogen dependent. An extra benefit of HRT is the reduction of incidence of coronary heart disease and, less consistently, stroke.

If HRT were recommended as a public health measure aimed at reducing the incidence of 'osteoporotic fractures' it would need to be acceptable to the generality of women. Wallace and colleagues (1990) found an uptake of only 36% among women aged 50-70 offered HRT following a distal forearm fracture. Even in the age group 50-54 the uptake was only 54%. In the USA only 40% of women thought to be at above average risk for osteoporotic fractures were compliant with HRT after 6 to 12 months. Given present uptake of HRT, its encouragement as a public health measure aimed at reducing the incidence of 'osteoporotic fractures' seems unlikely to have a major effect and population screening using currently available measures of bone density measurement is not justifiable. However, bone density measurements do have a place in the clinical assessment of someone who is of apparently high risk of osteoporotic fracture for other reasons. Indications might include an early menopause, an 'osteoporotic fracture' such as of the distal forearm, and a family history of osteoporosis. Facilities should be available for such clinical use of densitometry.

HRT needs to be investigated further, in particular the issue of whether it produces long-term or only temporary benefits. It seems that long-term large randomised controlled trials are both justified and necessary. The public should be educated in the need for trials and encouraged to participate.

Fluoride

There is no consistent evidence linking the prevalence of osteoporosis or the incidence of osteoporosis-related fractures with the fluoride content of drinking water (Gordon and Corbin 1992). Water fluoridation to levels of around 1mg/l currently being advocated for the prevention of dental caries would be unlikely to have an impact on UK hip fracture incidence.

Physical activity

Exercise protects against PFF (Law, Wald and Meade 1991); compared with women with low levels of activity, moderate activity confers a 40-50% lower risk and high levels a 70% lower risk. Benefits are perhaps mediated by reducing falls or improving protective responses as well as improving bone strength. A recent study by Prince and colleagues (1991) concluded that postmenopausal bone loss could be slowed by an exercise regime associated with either HRT or with dietary calcium supplementation. The exercise-HRT regime was the more effective but caused more side-effects.

Low body weight

Osteoporosis is associated with low body weight. This is presumably partly due to lower stress on bones but in postmenopausal women adipose tissue converts adrenal steroids into oestrogens. The hazards of being overweight probably cancel out the benefits on osteoporosis, so maintenance of average body weight seems the desirable aim.

Dietary calcium

The relevance of dietary calcium to osteoporosis remains unresolved. Epidemiological and clinical trial evidence suggests that dietary calcium intake in childhood can affect peak bone mass. It seems prudent to recommend dietary calcium intakes of the order of 800 to 1000mg/day for the population as a whole, but the scope for affecting fracture incidence through the manipulation of dietary calcium or the prescription of calcium supplements in adult life seems limited.

Cyclical etidronate therapy

Recent trials have shown that cyclical etidronate therapy has a beneficial effect on spinal bone density and the incidence of vertebral fractures (Storm and colleagues 1990; Watts and colleagues 1990; Miller and colleagues 1991). So far the studies have been over periods of the order of two years and longer term work is needed. Nonetheless etidronate therapy is coming into use in the UK as its profile of adverse effects is low and it avoids the problems of HRT in older women. It is too early to assess its ultimate role in prevention.

7.3   Incontinence

Incontinence of urine or faeces is an affliction with a wide range of severity. Estimates of its prevalence are therefore critically dependent on definition and methods of estimation. It is also a socially humiliating affliction that many sufferers are unwilling to acknowledge even to their medical or nursing advisers. This fact adds to the difficulties in estimating prevalence rates and evaluating treatment.

7.3.1   Urinary incontinence

There are several different types of urinary incontinence and mixed forms are common in later life. Acute incontinence can occur in a number of situations including urinary infections, immobilising or delirious illnesses and epilepsy. We are concerned here with chronic or established incontinence which is either continuous or recurrent. Table 7.3 offers one classification of the main forms of established urinary incontinence. Of these stress and urge incontinence are the commonest in the third age.

In a recent survey conducted by the Oxford Regional Health Authority, approximately 90% of people aged 65 to 74 claimed never to have episodes of urinary incontinence and 96% never to suffer from faecal incontinence (Oxford Regional Health Authority 1991). A postal survey of people registered with 12 general practices distributed throughout the country revealed rather higher prevalence rates of urinary incontinence as shown in table 7.4 (Thomas and colleagues 1980).

Table 7.3

Forms of chronic urinary incontinence.

Stress	loss or urine on coughing or straining
Urge	often due to precipitate bladder contractions
Overflow	secondary to obstruction of bladder outflow
Fistulous	e.g. fistula between bladder and vagina
Functional	difficulty in getting to toilet
Disinhibitory	occurs in some forms of brain damages
Behavioural	(rare) form of social manipulation

Table 7.4

Percentage prevalence of occasional, regular and 'uncertain' urinary incontinence.

age group	Men			Women		
	Occasional	Regular	Uncertain	Occasional	Regular	Uncertain
45-54	3.7	1.6	1.4	21.9	11.8	2.4
55-64	5.7	2.9	2.6	18.6	11.9	2.8
65-74	8.4	6.1	4.9	14.6	8.8	3.4
75-84	9.5	8.1	7.0	13.6	16.0	7.2

(*Source:* Thomas and colleagues 1980)

Stress incontinence was commonest in women at ages 45 to 54 while urge incontinence increased in prevalence with age up to 64. Stress incontinence became less common in later life. At ages under 65 the prevalence rates reported in this survey were lower than those found in some other studies where rates in women of over 40% have been reported (Jolleys 1988). Among women there was an association of incontinence with parity. Incontinence rates were lowest among the childless and highest among women with four or more births.

In men in the third age urinary incontinence is often associated with prostatic hypertrophy. Although pharmacological approaches to this problem are being developed, surgical resection of all or part of the enlarged gland remains a very common treatment option. The type of and indications for surgery vary between centres and countries, and there is considerable doubt about some aspects of its effectiveness in reducing symptoms and morbidity. Systematic research is urgently needed (Fowler and colleagues 1988).

7.3.2 Faecal and double incontinence

Faecal incontinence is likely to be subject to an even greater degree of under-reporting than is urinary incontinence. Thomas and colleagues (1984) have estimated the prevalence of faecal or double incontinence based on a report of two or more episodes in the preceding month. Overall 11% of men over 65 and 13% of women were faecally or doubly incontinent. Only 44% of the cases identified were known to the health and social services and 71% of these were resident in institutions.

Faecal and double incontinence are associated with a range of anorectal and neurological disorders. In later life the commonest cause is rectal or colonic overloading due to constipation. In middle-aged women a pelvic neuropathy, sometimes possibly a consequence of childbirth, is a cause of faecal incontinence which may be improved by surgical intervention. Any form of chronic diarrhoea will also lead to incontinence in a proportion of cases.

7.3.3 Management of incontinence

In a subsample of 158 people reporting urinary incontinence in the survey by Thomas and colleagues (1980) and who gave interviews, 22% had moderate or severe incontinence but only a third of these were receiving help from the health or social services for their incontinence. Recent reviews by Ouslander (1990) of urinary incontinence in elderly people, and by Cardozo (1991) of urinary incontinence in women, suggest that many sufferers do not receive what is thought to be the best care that is available. This is partly to be due to inadequate training of health and social service workers. A variety of training materials have been devised to overcome this problem and the great majority of professionals are reported to have an interest in updating their training in continence work. It has been suggested, however, that 'the referral process may need to be opened up to sidestep uncommitted practitioners' (Social Policy Research Unit 1989).

One reason for the lack of enthusiasm among medical professionals, and an important general issue in the management of incontinence, is the inadequacy of evaluation of many of the treatments currently deployed. This is particularly true for surgical approaches to the management of stress incontinence and to incontinence associated with early prostatic hypertrophy in men. A range of operative procedures are in common use and each surgeon is convinced of the efficacy of whatever technique he or she applies. This prevents the use of randomised controlled clinical trials to compare techniques. One way of overcoming this problem would be by a process of randomised allocation of patients to surgeons but so far the administrative difficulties associated with this approach have not been overcome. Most of the evaluations of treatment of incontinence, including surgical, behavioural, pharmacological and physiotherapy techniques have been uncontrolled or short-term or both. Newer techniques including neurostimulatory implants are under development, particularly for victims of neurological disorders, but are unlikely to prove generally applicable to the majority of incontinent people in the population.

The cost of deploying what on present opinion would be adequate services for incontinent patients was calculated in 1987 as not less than £270,000 for a typical health district (population 250,000) with an estimated 40% for the unrecognised cases (Townsend 1988). How much of the cost might be offset by reduced rates of institutionalisation and prosthetic costs is unclear, but without better evidence on efficacy health authorities might question outlays of this order. At present there seems to be a major need for a coordinated and systematic approach to the evaluation of methods of ascertainment, assessment and management of incontinence in the population.

8 MENTAL WELLBEING

8.1   Problems of adjustment

In numerical terms more unhappiness in middle age (as at all ages) arises from problems of adjustment than from mental disease. Women experience the menopause which, in some instances, is associated with distressing physical changes and spontaneous mood changes. Furthermore the menopause may carry psychosocial implications in self-perception and change of role.

In men, though there are some minor changes in sex hormone secretion in middle life, there is no physiological discontinuity corresponding to the menopause. Paradoxically, however, the psychological stress associated with the transition from second to third age may be greater in men. There are many reasons for this. In modern Western society the role of the older man is not as well defined nor as biologically useful as that of the older woman as grandmother or aunt which involve her practically in the present and psychologically in the future. The social function of a man is often centred on his roles as doer and provider, neither of which may outlive his employment. The discharge of these roles during his working life may leave no time for the development of other interests which could have provided reasons for living in his retirement.

Anxieties and uncertainties about sexual activity may affect both men and women in the third age. Medical reasons that necessitate the ending of sexual activity are rare before the eighth decade of life and there is increasing recognition that such activity remains fully appropriate as long as it continues to be desired.

In times of social change both men and women may come to feel alienated from a world in which they seem to have no place, in which the ideals they have lived for are despised and the labours of their early lives are undervalued. The stresses induced by such disjointing of the personal world contribute not only to the well-recognised phenomenon of the 'midlife crisis' but also to a more chronic *Weltschmertz* or 'existential neurosis' that precludes contentment and corrodes social relationships. Doctors recognise this phenomenon and often have to address it in the counselling of individual patients for whom it is increasing the burden of more specifically medical problems. As a widespread source of unhappiness in the third age it merits more systematic attention. It is not generally seen as primarily a health issue but in contemporary British society it is difficult to identify a more appropriate context within which it could be considered.

8.2   Depression

Depression has been called the epidemic of old age being one of the most common conditions found in surveys of older persons (Brayne and Ames 1988). However, it has proved difficult to quantify prevalence accurately. Depression is an umbrella term, referring to a continuum that extends from the normal reactions of sadness at life's adverse events through to major disorders for which there are strict diagnostic criteria. In addition, depression can often accompany and be secondary to other psychiatric disorders such as dementia. All depressions have features in common such as deflated mood, increased worry, apathy or tension but severity and combinations of symptoms are extremely variable. There is no best method of classifying depressive disorders and rates will vary greatly according to where the "cutoff" point for classifying a person as depressed is placed. A second source of discrepancy lies in the methodology used to gather data. Studies that have used clinical diagnostic criteria (such as an interview with a psychiatrist) yield lower prevalence rates than those which use self-report questionnaires which encompass a broader definition of depression. Use of different questionnaires also adds to difficulties in making comparisons.

There appear to be no consistent age trends for prevalence of depression in older persons, some studies suggesting an increased prevalence with advancing age whereas others show a decline. There appears to be no satisfactory study which compares the prevalence of depression across the entire lifespan, such studies as have been reported having too few older subjects for the results to be meaningful. Studies specifically looking at those aged 65 or over provide more data but it is then difficult to make comparisons with younger age groups. Furthermore, longitudinal (or prospective) studies are scarce. Such studies need to be carried out in order to eliminate the possible confounding of age with cohort effects. For example, there been some indication that certain cohorts have been protected against depressive symptoms, which could possibly introduce an artefactual age effect in cross-sectional comparisons (Blazer and colleagues 1991). Bearing these difficulties in mind, table 8.1 lists the results from two studies where smaller age-band data are provided. It is difficult to discern any clear pattern. For males, there appears to be a steady increase in prevalence with advancing age. However, the situation appears more mixed for females, with rates decreasing in "early" old age before increasing once more. There is, perhaps, a clearer pattern between the sexes, many

Table 8.1

Percentage prevalence of depression by age groups in Kentucky and London.

age group	men	women
Kentucky		
55-59	13.2	19.0
60-64	11.1	15.0
65-74	12.9	14.5
75+	17.5	26.0
London		
65-69	13.6	21.4
70-74	13.3	16.5

(*Sources:* Kentucky, Murrell and colleagues 1983; London, Livingston and colleagues 1990)

studies finding somewhat higher overall rates of depression amongst women. Women, however, appear to report milder depression more commonly than men (Kay and colleagues 1964).

8.2.1   Risk Factors for Depression

Advanced age, per se, may not necessarily be the predominant risk factor for depression. Changes in prevalence rates for depression could result from a relative increase in the distribution of other risk factors known to be associated with depression which are more common in later years. These include a previous history of depression, physical illness and disability, recent life events (such as bereavement) and social and economic circumstances. Indeed, Blazer and colleagues (1991) found that after taking into account such factors as physical disability, social support and income, a previously positive association between age and depressive symptoms disappeared. Murphy (1982) provides some evidence that the risk factors are additive, poor health and deprived social circumstances increasing the risk of depression following a major life event.

Illness and disability

There is a well-established association between physical illness and depression. Murrell and colleagues (1983) found that depression increased with poor health and that this relationship was unaffected by age in both sexes. Likewise, depressive symptoms are often reported by patients with chronic pain. In the UK, the Health and Lifestyle Survey (Huppert and colleagues 1987) found that self-reporting of symptoms of physical illness was correlated with higher scores for psychiatric illness. Turner and Noh (1988) reported that the disabled have three times the risk of depression (35% vs 12%) than the non-disabled. Often it is difficult to distinguish between physical illness and depression as there are symptoms which are common to both. For example, many scales used to assess depressive symptoms contain several questions concerning somatic complaints, such as loss of appetite, sleeplessness and lack of energy. Higher scores on depression scales, therefore, may reflect declining physical health rather than a depressed mood state.

Life Events

Murphy (1982) reported that depressed patients had experienced significantly more "severe" life events than healthy subjects in the previous year. The most frequent of such events in the patients were physical illness and the separation or death of a spouse or child. Bereavement and loss are common occurrences in the older person's life and these are considered to be important risk factors, and have been shown to lead to a six-fold elevation in depressive symptomatology in widows at one month post-bereavement (Harlow and colleagues 1991). However, such losses by themselves are not usually sufficient to cause long-term depression, indeed depression rates observed in later life are remarkably low given the increased prevalence of bereavement. The majority of older people cope well with their losses. Thus other risk factors must operate in addition to the bereavement.

Social Factors

Social circumstance appears to be a strong predictor of depression. Murphy (1982) found that whereas none of a sample classified as "middle" class were depressed, 17 of those classed as "working" class were. Furthermore, "working" class members suffered a higher rate of severe life events, social difficulties and health problems, sufficient to account for the increased prevalence of depression. Lack of a confiding relationship may be important in increasing vulnerability to depression. Murphy (1982) found that chances of developing a depression after a severe life event, without a confiding relationship were considerably higher than with one. A similar result was also obtained by Harlow and colleagues (1991) in their study of bereavement. Other studies have also highlighted the importance of social support in reducing vulnerability to depression (Brown and colleagues 1986, 1987). Feeling lonely (rather than living alone) has also been found to correlate with depression (Evans and colleagues 1991). Furthermore, the presence of a home help was negatively correlated with depression, indicating the important role that this service plays in meeting older persons physical and emotional needs.

8.3   Dementia

Dementia implies an acquired irreversible global impairment of cognitive function, ie all higher brain functions are impaired including memory, perception, attention and reasoning. Not all functions are necessarily affected to an equal degree at all stages and in the early stages of some dementias memory problems may be dominant. However, local brain damage can give memory problems without progression to dementia, so demonstration of global impairment is of crucial diagnostic importance. Demonstration of acquired cognitive impairment usually depends on reports from friends or relatives or may be deduced from a decline in occupational performance. Dementia is not the only cause of acquired impairment, however, and other problems such as depression and drug or alcohol abuse need to be excluded.

8.3.1   Causes of dementia

There are three main groups of dementia; commonest in the UK is Alzheimer's disease (AD). Second commonest is vascular dementia due to disease in the blood vessels supplying the brain, multi-infarct dementia (MID) being its usual form. It may prove difficult without invasive tests to distinguish between vascular dementia and AD in a particular patient, and mixed forms are not uncommon. The third, rarer group includes Huntington's disease, Pick's disease and Creutzfeld-Jakob disease which tend to follow more distinctive clinical courses.

8.3.2   The epidemiology of dementia

It is generally assumed that the epidemiology of MID follows that of stroke although there has been no clear demonstration that this is so. MID increases in incidence with age, affects men more than women and is related to high blood pressure, coronary heart disease and other risk factors for stroke. One may hope that if the incidence of stroke is falling, as seems likely, vascular dementia will follow suit. Furthermore, treatment with anticoagulants for people with atrial fibrillation is likely to prevent some cases of vascular dementia as well as bringing about a 30 to 40% reduction in the risk of stroke. Other approaches to preventing MID as distinct from stroke, for example by drugs claimed to increase brain blood flow, have not been convincing.

There are higher rates of dementia in the lower social classes and educational groups. There are possible explanations for this if it is a valid finding and not a test artefact. These groups may have been differentially exposed to some environmental cause of AD or they may have a higher prevalence of other forms of brain damage, such as vascular disease. Another possibility is that better brains, whether better because of their genetic endowment or made to function better by education, can compensate better and longer for the damage caused by dementias. If so, even if the incidence and prevalence of brain damage do not change, improving the nutrition and education of the population may reduce the incidence and prevalence of mental and social impairments. In Sweden such improvements may indeed be occurring (Berg 1980); in Britain data are only available for younger age groups but are also encouraging (Lynn and Hampson 1986).

Prevalence rates have been averaged from published studies in Table 8.2 (Jorm 1990). Although rates for all types of dementia combined are broadly similar in the two sexes, the M:F ratios for prevalence rates of AD and MID are 0.5 and 1.8 respectively. Prevalence rates are determined partly by survival times which may be increasing in the UK, probably through improved nursing care (Blessed and Wilson 1982).

Table 8.2

Age-specific percentage prevalence rates of dementia (all forms).

Age group	Median age	Prevalence
60-64	62.5	0.7
65-69	67.5	1.4
70-74	72.5	2.8
75-79	77.5	5.6
80-84	82.0	10.5
85-89	87.0	20.8
90-95	91.5	38.6

(*Source:* Jorm 1990)

There are no third age incidence data for the UK, although an annual incidence of 1.4% has been reported for people 75 and over (Jagger and colleagues 1989). Hagnell and colleagues (1983) have presented data from the Lundby Study which is unusual in having made observations over a long period of time and in having involved an unusually wide age range (table 8.3). For the third age the cumulative risk of dementia is low and its horrors are largely reserved for later life. Dementia has a major impact on people in the third age in the burden of caring for more aged relatives with the condition.

Table 8.3

Incidence rates per 1000/year for AD and MID in Lundby 1957-72.

Age	Men AD	Men MID	Women AD	Women MID
0-49	0.0	0.0	0.0	0.0
50-59	0.0	0.4	0.0	0.0
60-69	0.9	4.1	1.7	1.3
70-79	7.0	4.4	12.3	5.1
80-89	18.9	20.5	25.3	9.3
90-99	13.2	40.2	17.8	0.0

(*Source:* Hagnell and colleagues 1983)

8.3.3 Alzheimer's disease

Care

There is no known cure for AD. Well designed care offers a pattern of supportive services both to the victim and to his or her informal carers. There are many uncertainties about the best pattern; not least are questions about the appropriate balance between domiciliary and institutional care. These uncertainties apply to respite care, in which the victim is admitted to a hospital or residential home for short periods to provide carers with a rest. In some cases the disorientation and anxiety induced in the victim may outweigh the benefits to carers. The Medical Research Council has funded an observational study of the effectiveness of patterns of care currently being provided in four centres. However, there will be a need for continuing interventive studies based on hypotheses arising from this work.

Causes of Alzheimer's disease

The causes of AD are still unknown. A general model for the disease is that the brain damage results from interaction between one or more environmental agents and a genetic susceptibility (Grimley Evans 1992). Most people can live out a long life without accumulating enough damage to become demented but a minority have an unfortunate genetic endowment and accumulate damage faster. Thus a genetic component is more readily recognised in early-onset than in late-onset disease. For methodological reasons it has been difficult to detect geographical or occupational differences in the incidence of

AD which might lead to the identification of possible environmental causes and it is possible that these might prove to be ubiquitous. There is a study under way in five British centres comparing the incidence of AD in northern, southern, rural and urban settings.

Possible causative factors currently receiving attention include aluminium (Mortimer and colleagues 1985) and parental age of birth (Jorm 1990). In the absence of a clear cut lead it is important to continue the present comprehensive programmes of research into the genes that cause AD and their mechanisms of action, environmental influences and optimal patterns of care.

9 PREVALENCE OF MAJOR RISK FACTORS IN THE THIRD AGE

9.1 Alcohol

Alcohol is a major cause of premature deaths, perhaps 28,000/year in England and Wales (Anderson 1988), also contributing to public disorder, violence, family disputes, child neglect, road accidents, fire, drowning, accidents in the home and employment problems (Faculty of Public Health Medicine 1991). Mortality from liver cirrhosis is strongly linked to alcohol consumption (Anderson 1991). Alcohol is linked to cancer, increasing risks for cancer of the oral cavity, larynx and pharynx, also to strokes, hypertension and cardiovascular disease (Faculty of Public Health Medicine 1991).

Some studies find abstainers and those drinking large amounts are at greater risk of death than moderate drinkers suggesting that moderate alcohol consumption has a protective effect, notably on ischaemic heart disease (Marmot and colleagues 1981). Confounding this association, some abstainers may have stopped drinking as a result of pre-existing disease which contributes to their higher mortality rates (Shaper and colleagues 1988).

9.1.1 Estimates of consumption of alcohol

Consumption in England and Wales rose steadily from the 1950s, tailing off in the 1980s and 90s, with average consumption per person estimated as 9.6-9.8 litres of pure alcohol per person per year (Anderson 1991). Individual intakes are subject to under-reporting, particularly if heavy. However, the 1988 General Household Survey found that 27% of men and 11% of women drink more than 21 and 14 units of alcohol per week respectively (1 unit = 8 grams alcohol), the recommended "sensible" limits (OPCS 1988). Smaller proportions of the older population drink heavily (table 9.1). Changes between national surveys in 1978 and 1987 show consumption falling among younger men, but increasing among older men and all women except the youngest. However, overall weekly consumption was unchanged at 19.5 units for men compared with 7.2 units for women (Goddard 1991).

9.1.2 Action on alcohol

Alcohol-related disease rates reflect population levels of alcohol consumption (Kendell 1984a). Thus, in England and Wales from 1979 to 1982, consumption fell by 11% whilst there was a decline of alcoholism admissions (19%), cirrhosis mortality (4%), drunkenness convictions (16%) and drink-driving convictions (7%) (Kendell 1984b).

Table 9.1

Percentage prevalence by sex and age for levels of alcohol consumption (units per week), England and Wales 1988.

Alcohol consumption	18-24	25-44	45-64	65+
Men				
Non drinker	5	4	7	14
Very low (below 1)	6	5	11	19
Low (1-10)	30	33	37	40
Moderate (11-21)	24	25	21	14
Fairly high (22-35)	15	16	11	8
High (36-50)	9	9	6	3
Very high (51+)	11	9	6	2
Women				
Non drinker	8	7	12	23
Very low (below 1)	12	18	27	37
Low (1-7)	42	44	41	29
Moderate (8-14)	21	18	12	7
Fairly high (15-25)	10	9	6	3
High (26-35)	4	2	2	1
Very high (36+)	3	2	1	0

(*Source:* General Household Survey 1988)

It is clearly beneficial to reduce consumption of alcohol. Although consumption is influenced by cultural/religious traditions, advertising and health promotion, availability seems crucial. During the First World War, beer consumption was reduced by 63% and spirits by 52% by reducing outlets and opening hours (Smart 1974). Price powerfully influences consumption (Semple and Yarrow 1974, Popham and colleagues 1975; table 9.2) and raising duties, based strictly on alcohol content, is the obvious means to reduce consumption (Cook 1982). The UK Treasury suggests that a 1% rise in the real price of alcohol leads to a fall in consumption of beer by 0.25%, spirits 1.5% and wine 1% (Faculty of Public Health Medicine 1991). Following real rises in duty in UK in 1981, alcohol consumption by "regular drinkers" fell by 18% and their "adverse effects score" fell by 16% (Kendell and colleagues 1983). Unfortunately, European Common Market harmonisation may oblige the Government to reduce our higher taxes on alcohol (especially wine) potentially increasing UK consumption by 46%, doubling numbers drinking 50 units/week (Maynard and O'Brien 1982, Baker and McKay 1990). As the frequency of alcohol-related problems would rise, Government should resist harmonisation proposals which significantly reduce the price of alcohol (Faculty of Public Health Medicine 1991).

Table 9.2

Consumption of alcohol and its relative price, Ontario, Canada, 1928-67.

year	consumption (1/yr)	relative price
1928	2.81	291
1931	2.64	320
1934	2.09	391
1937	3.36	246
1940	3.64	211
1943	4.91	183
1946	5.82	197
1949	7.18	166
1952	7.32	146
1955	7.55	134
1958	7.96	123
1961	8.14	123
1964	8.73	111
1967	8.91	100

(*Source:* Popham, Schmidt and de Lint 1975)

9.2   Smoking

The serious health hazards of smoking are underlined by the reports of the Royal College of Physicians (1962, 1971 and 1977). Smoking is associated with increased morbidity and mortality from cancer (particularly of the lung, mouth, larynx and oesophagus), ischaemic heart disease, gastric and duodenal ulcers and chronic bronchitis.

Data on smoking in the UK are provided by the annual General Household Survey (OPCS) from 1972 onwards and the Tobacco Advisory Council (Wald and Nicolandes-Bowman 1990) from 1948 onwards, the latter tending to indicate greater prevalence rates reflecting differences in methodology. However, changes over time in the two surveys are remarkably consistent. Prevalence of cigarette smoking is lower in the third age (table 9.3) and is greatest in 20-30 year olds. Since the 1970s the prevalence of smoking has been declining for both men and women across all age groups. Women previously had lower rates but prevalence has fallen more in men, reducing the differences. Current trends would suggest a prevalence rate of around 20% in men over 60, and 15% in women over 60 in ten years from now.

Weekly cigarette consumption per smoker relates to age in both sexes, those over 60 smoking less than other groups except those aged 16-19 (table 9.4). There have been slight upward trends in weekly cigarette consumption per smoker since the 1970s.

Table 9.3

The current percentage prevalence of cigarette smoking in the UK.

Age	Men	Women
16-19	28	32
20-24	38	39
25-34	36	34
35-49	34	33
50-59	28	29
60+	24	20

(*Source:* OPCS Monitor/GHS 1990)

Table 9.4

Current average weekly cigarette consumption per smoker in the UK.

Age	Men	Women
16-19	89	80
20-24	110	92
25-34	115	103
35-49	135	106
50-59	121	107
60+	106	81

(*Source:* OPCS Monitor/GHS 1990)

9.3   Obesity

Being overweight increases health risks, particularly for adult onset diabetes, hypertension, ischaemic heart disease, certain cancers, gout, gall bladder disease and arthritis (Royal College of Physicians 1983). Body Mass Index (BMI), the ratio of weight in kilograms to height in metres squared, is generally used to define obesity; levels are: ‹20 for underweight, 25-30 for overweight and ›30 for obesity. In British men aged 40-59 years, mortality rates increased with BMI for values greater than 28, excess deaths being mainly cardiovascular (Wannamethee and Shaper 1989). However, in the large

Whitehall Study risks altered with age (Lichenstein and colleagues 1985). In men 50-60 years there was increased risk with obesity which disappeared over 60 but one for excessively lean men appeared (Jarrett and colleagues 1982). There is a lack of data for women.

Table 9.5 presents the distribution of BMI in the population derived from two recent national studies (OPCS 1990, Allied Dunbar National Fitness Survey 1992). Overweight is commonest at older ages with 62% of men 55-64 and 78% of women 65-74 overweight. Furthermore, adult obesity is increasing in all age groups (OPCS 1981, 1987) with average BMI for adults 16-64 increasing from 24.3 to 24.9 in men and from 23.9 to 24.6 in women over the six years.

Table 9.5

Percentage distribution of Body Mass Index (BMI) across age groups.

age & sex	underweight BMI ‹20	normal BMI 20-25	overweight BMI 25-30	obese BMI ›30
males				
16-24	15	64	18	3
25-34	4	60	30	6
35-49	4	44	41	11
50-64	5	33	53	9
females				
16-24	25	52	17	6
25-34	17	56	16	11
35-49	8	52	30	10
50-64	5	49	28	18

(*Source:* Dietary and Nutritional Survey of British Adults, OPCS)

9.4   Blood Cholesterol Levels

High levels of cholesterol in the blood are a risk factor in cardiovascular disease with high levels of the low density lipoprotein (LDL) fraction being strongly adverse whilst the high density lipoprotein fraction (HDL) is protective (OPCS 1990). Serum cholesterol levels from the Diet and Nutrition Survey of British Adults (OPCS 1990) are shown in table 9.6. Total serum cholesterol increased with age. At young ages levels are higher in men than in women but increases in women around ages 50-64 reverses the sex difference in later life. LDL cholesterol shows similar rises with age (OPCS 1990).

Table 9.6

Percentage distribution of total serum cholesterol values (mmol/l) across age groups.

cholesterol	‹5.2	5.2-6.4	6.4-7.8	›7.8
males				
18-24	75	21	4	0
25-34	41	43	12	4
35-49	21	45	25	9
50-64	13	45	32	10
females				
18-24	66	28	4	2
25-34	61	37	1	1
35-49	35	44	18	3
50-64	10	31	38	21

(*Source:* Dietary and Nutritional Survey of British Adults, OPCS, 1990)

Dietary cholesterol has little effect on serum cholesterol, the major determinants being total fat consumption and the ratio of saturated and polyunstaturated acids in the fat. A high ratio of polyunsaturated to saturated fats (P:S ratio) is advantageous. Table 9.7 summarises fat and cholesterol intakes. There was no difference in the proportions of total food energy derived from fat across the age groups but a lower P:S ratio at higher ages. Data from the National Food Survey (Chesher 1990) suggest that whereas the energy derived from fat has decreased slightly, the P:S ratio has risen over the last decade, though these advantageous changes are less at older ages.

9.5   Blood Pressure

Raised blood pressure levels increase the risk of cardiovascular and cerebrovascular disease and in the developed world there is an increase in blood pressure with age (Whelton and Klag 1989). Table 9.8 shows UK data, systolic and diastolic blood pressure increasing with age for both sexes. Prevalence of untreated hypertension rises to a peak in the third age. Hypertension is more common in men than women up until the third age, whereupon the situation reverses (table 9.9). There are no UK data on secular trends for blood pressure. As to effectiveness of hypertensive therapy, of those aged over 60 on treatment, some 22% of men and 30% of women remained hypertensive (Cox and colleagues 1987). It is unclear how much of these findings represent non-compliance rather than lack of efficacy.

Table 9.7

Mean percentage of energy from fats, P:S ratios and cholesterol intakes.

	% energy from total fats	% energy from saturated fats	P:S ratio	cholesterol intake mg/day
males				
16-24	40.2	16.1	0.41	362
25-34	41.0	16.5	0.43	383
35-49	40.2	16.3	0.42	398
50-64	40.2	17.2	0.35	407
females				
16-24	39.8	16.4	0.40	247
25-34	40.7	16.9	0.39	264
35-49	40.3	16.9	0.38	295
50-64	40.3	17.5	0.35	294

(*Source:* Dietary and Nutritional Survey of British Adults, OPCS, 1990)

Table 9.8

Percentage distribution of blood pressure classes by age with those receiving drugs for hypertension excluded.

	systolic blood pressure mm Hg				diastolic blood pressure mm Hg			
	‹120	120-139	140-159	160+	‹75	75-84	85-94	95+
males								
18-24	58	41	1	0	71	22	7	0
25-34	40	53	6	1	48	36	13	3
35-49	35	48	14	3	35	35	20	10
50-64	19	56	19	6	20	42	29	9
females								
18-24	84	16	0	0	82	15	2	1
25-34	82	17	1	0	74	21	3	2
35-49	60	32	7	1	57	27	12	4
50-64	35	42	15	8	37	35	22	6

(*Source:* Dietary and Nutritional Survey of British Adults, OPCS, 1990)

Table 9.9

Percentage prevalence of hypertension by age (categories as defined by WHO).

	borderline hypertension	untreated hypertension	treated hypertension
males			
18-29	6	1	–
30-39	7	4	1
40-49	11	8	3
50-59	17	12	10
60-69	18	13	16
70-79	24	19	17
80+	23	11	16
females			
18-29	1	–	–
30-39	3	1	–
40-49	5	3	4
50-59	13	9	11
60-69	18	12	14
70-79	16	23	25
80+	20	15	23

(*Source:* Cox and colleagues 1987)

10 CONCLUSION

Our review of specific diseases suggests that the health of people in the third age will improve if present trends continue and people pursue healthy active lifestyles. A few factors can be identified which might interrupt these trends. One is the failure of cigarette smoking in young women to fall with its implications for cancer, vascular disease and osteoporosis in middle age and beyond. The second possibility that has to be borne in mind is that of a major epidemic of AIDS. The increasing numbers of people from ethnic minorities in the United Kingdom in the third age may also modify the overall optimistic picture in view of the higher rates of hypertensive and cardiovascular disease recorded in Afro-Caribbean and Asian groups. We also have to recognise the deleterious impact on health of poverty and unemployment, which may or may not be an increasing influence in the next decades.

If European Community legislation reduces the tax on alcohol, it is likely that there will be an increased toll of alcohol-related diseases affecting the British population. Analogous consequences would follow a reduction in the real price of cigarettes. European policy also has profound effects on the opportunities for a healthy diet.

Climatic change may also bring some deleterious effects, particularly in the incidence of skin cancer, consequent on increased ultraviolet radiation through disruption of the ozone layer. We also have to recognise that there may be other unpredictable environmental hazards or cultural changes in lifestyle that might slow down or reverse the present encouraging trends in third age health.

Our data also suggest an increase over time in the use of health services, probably reflecting increased expectations rather than increased morbidity but also an increase in the health interventions available. Improvements in health technology will increase the applicability of health interventions in older age groups. We would therefore not expect, at least in the medium term, the improved health of the third age population to be reflected in much diminution in health resource consumption.

It is not easy to predict the economic consequences of these trends of increasing health but with some increase in health resource consumption. It is facile to assume that increased longevity will inevitably lead to increased numbers of people reaching ages at which average health costs rise. In general, the later the onset of disabling disease the shorter the survival in a disabled state. Total costs per life year gained may therefore not correlate directly with average life expectancy. The framework within which economic analyses of this kind have to be made needs to be defined ideologically. Most citizens, we believe, would regard prevention of disabling diseases and prolongation of healthy life as good things and, from society's point of view, a good investment.

Older people have considerable scope for improving their own health by choice of lifestyle. To do this they need to be accurately informed and offered appropriate opportunities. Thought needs to be directed to the most effective means and settings for updating people's knowledge about healthy living. Employers might welcome involvement in programmes that improve the health of their employees whilst working and benefit their life in retirement.

We regard it as crucial that access of older people to the best of specialist medical care should be on the basis of physiological assessment, rather than age. There is already evidence of age discrimination in terms of access of older people to coronary care and thrombolysis (Dudley and Burns 1992). In the future there may be some dangers for older people in the new arrangements in the National Health Service. Overt age discrimination could arise if purchasing authorities negotiate contracts separately for different age groups. Covert age discrimination could arise if Hospital Trusts, being paid a flat rate for particular interventions, designate older people whose lengths of stay may be longer than average as "medically" unsuitable for intervention when the true determinant is their poorer profit margin. We fear that fiscal pressures will lead to such age discrimination unless case-mix specifications are rigorous and are monitored by specific audit. It should also be recognised that with the current trends in improvements in technology, interventions will become increasingly worthwhile at increasingly older ages. We are concerned that all those professionals who act as gatekeepers in the various parts of the health and social service system should recognise that older people should not be offered prosthetic care until all possibilities for therapeutic interventions have been explored. This is a message which particularly needs to be built into the training of social workers whose traditional orientation has been towards care rather than cure.

Finally, in the interactions between health and lifestyle it is important to recognise that social policies for work, education and activity have important effects on health. The Government's 'Health of the Nation' initiative offers mechanisms whereby such a strategy for the third age could be developed. The concept of what constitutes the "health budget" might be widened to include employment, housing, education and fiscal policy.

REFERENCES

AA Foundation for Road Safety Research (1988) Motoring and the older driver. Basingstoke, Hants

Allied Dunbar National Fitness Survey (1992) The Sports Council, London

Anderson P (1991) Alcohol as a key area. British Medical Journal, 303;766-9

Anderson JJ, Felson DT (1988) Factors associated with osteoarthritis of the knee in the First National Health and Nutrition Examination Survey (HANES I): evidence for an association with weight, race and physical demands of work. Am J Epidemiol, 128;179-89

Anderson P (1988) Excess mortality associated with alcohol consumption. British Medical Journal, 297;824-7

Archea JC (1985) Environmental factors associated with stair accidents by the elderly. Clin Geriat med, 1;555-68

Astrand PO (1986) Comment on recommendations to follow for good physical fitness Acta Medica Scandinavica, 711(suppl);241-242

Baker P, McKay S (1990) The structure of alcohol taxes. A hangover from the past. IFS Commentary no 21. Institute for Fiscal Studies, London

Bamford J et al (1990) A prospective study of acute cerebrovascular disease in the community; the Oxfordshire community stroke project 1981-1986; 2 Incidence, case fatality rates and overall outcome at one year of cerebral infarction, primary intracerebral haemorrhage and subarachnoid heamorrhage. J Neurol Neurosurg Psychiat, 53;16-22

Barker DJP, Osmond C (1986) Childhood respiratory infection and adult chronic bronchitis in England and Wales. Br Med J 293;1271-5

Barker DJP, Osmond C (1986) Infant mortality, childhood nutrition, and ischaemic heart disease in England and Wales. Lancet, 1;1077-81

Barker DJP, Osmond C, Winter PD et al (1989) Weight in infancy and death from ischaemic heart disease. Lancet, 2;577-80

Barker DJP, Osmond C, Golding J, Kuh D, Wadsworth MEJ (1989) Growth in utero, blood pressure in childhood and adult life, and mortality from cardiovascular disease. Brit Med J, 298;564-7

Barker DJP (1991) The intrauterine origins of cardiovascular and obstructive lung disease in adult life. J Roy Coll Physns Lond, 25;129-33

Barker DJP, Meade TW, Fall CDH, Lee A et al (1992) Relation of fetal and infant growth to plasma fibrinogen and factor VII concentrations in adult life. Br Med J, 304;148-52

Barker DJP, Martyn CN (1992) The maternal and fetal origins of cardiovascular disease. J Epidemiol & Community Health, 46;8-11

Bassey EJ, Bendall MJ, Pearson M (1988) Muscle strength in the triceps surae and objectively measured customary walking activity in men and women over 65 years of age. Clinical Science, 74;85-9

Bassey EJ (1978) Age, Inactivity and some physiological responses to exercise Gerontology, 24;66-77

Bassey EJ, Fiatarone M, O'Neil E, Kelly M, Evans W, Lipsitz LA (1992) Leg Extensor power and functional performance in very old men and women Clinical Science, 82;321-327

Bebbington AC (1988) The expectation of life without disability in England and Wales, Soc Sci Med 27;321-6

Bebbington AC (1991) The expectation of life without disability in England and Wales; 1976-88 Population Trends, 66;26-9

Belbin E (1958) Methods of training older workers. Ergonomics, 1;207-21

Berg S (1980) Psychological functioning in 70- and 75-year-old people. Acta Psychiatr Scand. 288(suppl);

Blaxter M (1990) Health and lifestyles. Tavistock Routledge, London

Blazer D et al (1991) The association of age and depression among the elderly; an epidemiologic exploration. Journal of Gerontology, 46:210-215

Blessed G, Wilson ID (1982) The contemporary natural history of mental disorder in old age. Br J Psychiat, 141;59-67.

Bonita R (1992) Epidemiology of stroke. Lancet, 339;342-4.

Boyce WJ, Vessey MP (1985) Rising incidence of fracture of the proximal femur. Lancet, 1;150-1

Brayne C, Ames D (1988) The epidemiology of mental disorders in old age. in Mental health problems in old age, eds B Gearing, M Johnson and T Heller, Wiley, Chichester, pp10-26

Broderick JP, Phillips SJ, Whisnant JP, O'Fallon WM, Bergstrahl EJ (1989) Incidence rates of stroke in the eighties; the end of the decline in stroke? Stroke, 20;577-82

Brooks DN (1985) Factors relating to the under-use of postaural hearing aids. British Journal of Audiology, 19;211-7.

Broughton J (1987) Casualty rates by age and sex. in Road Accidents of Great Britain 1987: the casualty report, HMSO, London, pp60-4

Brown B, Bowman K (1987) Sensitivity to changes in size and velocity in young and elderly observers. Perception, 16;41-7

Brown GW, Bifulco A, Harris TO (1987) Life events, vulnerability and onset of depression. British Journal of Psychiatry, 150;30-42

Brown GW et al (1986) Social support, self-esteem and depression. Psychological Medicine, 16;813-831

Burg A (1967) Light sensitivity as related to age and sex. Perceptual and Motor Skills, 24;1279-88.

Burg A (1968) Lateral field as related to age and sex. Journal of Applied Psychology, 52;10-5.

Burrows B, Knudson J, Cline MG, Lebowitz D (1988) A reexamination of risk factors for ventilatory impairment. Amer Rev Respir Dis, 138;829-36

Campbell AJ, Borrie MJ, Spears GF, Jackson SL, Brown JS, Fitzgerald JL (1990) Circumstances and consequences of falls experienced by a community population of 70 years and over during a prospective study. Age Ageing, 19;136-41

Cardozo L (1991) Urinary incontinence in women; have we anything new to offer? Brit Med J, 303;1453-7

Carr D et al (1992) The effect of age on driving skills. Journal of the American Geriatrics Society, 40;567-73

Cerella J (1985) Information processing rates in the elderly. Psychological Bulletin, 98;67-83

Chesher A (1990) Changes in the nutritional content of British household food supplies during the 1980s. in Household food consumption and expenditure 1989, Annual report of the National Food Survey Committee. HMSO, London

Colley JRT, Douglas JWB, Reid DD (1973) Respiratory disease in young adults; influence of early childhood lower respiratory tract illness, social class, air pollution, and smoking. Br Med J, 3;195-8

Colvez A, Blanchet M (1981) Disability trends in the United States population 1966-76; analysis of reported causes. Am J Public Health, 71;464-71

Colvez A, Blanchet M (1983) Potential gains in life expectancy free of disability; a tool for health planning. Int J Epidemiol, 12;224-9

Cook PJ (1982) Alcohol taxes as a public health measure. British Journal of Addiction, 77;245-50

Cooper PJ (1990) Elderly drivers' views of self and driving in reaction to the evidence of accident data. Journal of Safety Research, 21;103-13

Cox BD, Blaxter M, Buckle ALJ et al (1987) The health and lifestyle survey. Health Promotion Trust, London

Craik FIM (1977) Age differences in human memory. in Handbook of the psychology of aging, eds JE Birren and KW Schaie, Van Nostrand Reinhold, New York, pp384-420

Crimmins EM, Saito Y, Ingegneri D (1989) Changes in life expectancy and disability-free life expectancy in the United States. Population & Development Review, 15;235-67

Dallosso HM, Morgan K, Bassey EJ, Ebrahim SBJ, Fentem PH, Arie THD (1988) Levels of customary activity among the old and the very old living at home Journal of Epidemiology and Community Health, 42;121-127

Davies DR, Parasuraman R (1982) The psychology of vigilance, Academic Press, London

Davies DR, Matthews D, Wong SK (1991) Ageing and work. in International review of industrial and organizational psychology, eds CI Cooper and IT Robertson, Vol. 6, John Wiley, Chichester, pp149-211

Davis AC (1989) The prevalence of hearing impairment and reported hearing disability among adults in Great Britain. International Journal of Epidemiology, 18;911-7.

Davis AC (1991) Epidemiological profile of hearing impairments: the scale and nature of the problem with special reference to the elderly. Acta Otolaryngologica, 476(Suppl);23-31.

Davis AC, Ostri B, Parving A (1991) Longitudinal study of hearing. Acta Otolaryngol 476(Suppl);12-22.

Davis AC et al (1992) Hearing impairments in middle age: the acceptability, benefit and cost of detection (ABCD). British Journal of Audiology, 26;1-14.

Doll R, Gray R, Hafner B, Peto R (1980) Mortality in relation to smoking; 22 years' observations on female British doctors. Br Med J, 1;967-71

Doll R, Peto R (1976) Mortality in relation to smoking; 20 years' observations on male British doctors. Br Med J, 2;1525-36

Dudley NJ, Burns E (1992) The influence of age on policies for admission and thrombolysis in coronary care units in the United Kingdom. Age and Ageing, 21;95-98

Edwards KE, Larson EB (1992) Benefits of exercise for older adults. Clinics in Geriatric Medicine, 8;35-50

Elias PK et al (1987) Acquisition of word-processing skills by younger, middle-age and older adults. Psychology and Aging, 2;340-8

Evans ME et al (1991) Depression in the elderly in the community; effect of physical illness and selected social factors. International Journal of Geriatric Psychiatry, 6;787-95

Faculty of Public Health Medicine of the Royal College of Physicians (1991) Alcohol and Public Health. Macmillan, London

Fall CHD, Barker DJP, Osmond C, Winter PD, Clark PMS, Hales CN (1992) The relation of infant feeding to adult serum cholesterol and death from ischaemic heart disease. Brit Med J, 304;801-5

Felson DT (1988) Epidemiology of hip and knee osteoarthritis. Epidem Rev, 10;1-28

Felson DT, Anderson JJ, Naimark A, et al (1988) Obesity and knee osteoarthritis. Ann Int Med, 109;18-24

Felson DT, Anderson JJ, Naimark A, et al (1989) Does smoking protect against osteoarthritis? Arthritis Rheum, 32;166-72

Felson DT, Anderson JJ, Naimark A, et al (1989) The prevalence of chondrocalcinosis in the elderly and its association with knee osteoarthritis; the Framingham Study. J Rheumatol, 16;1241-1245

Felson DT, Zhang Y, Anthony JM, Naimark A, Anderson JL (1992) Weight loss reduces the risk for symptomatic knee osteoarthritis in women. The Framingham Study. Ann Int Med, 116;535-39

Flynn JR (1984) The mean IQ of Americans: massive gains 1932-1978. Psychological Bulletin, 95;29-51

Flynn JR (1987) Massive IQ gains in 14 nations: what IQ tests really measure. Psychological Bulletin, 101;171-191

Fowler FJ, Wennberg J, Timothy RP et al (1988) Symptom status and quality of life following prostatectomy. JAMA 259:3018-22

Fozard JL (1990) Vision and hearing in aging. in Handbook of the psychology of aging, 3rd ed. (eds. JE Birren and KW Schaie), Academic Press, San Diego, pp.150-70.

Frankel S, Williams M, Nanchahal K, Coast J (1990) DHA Project; Epidemiologically based needs assessment. Report 2; total hip and knee joint replacement. Health Care Evaluation Unit, University of Bristol, Bristol

Fries J (1980) Aging, natural death and the compression of morbidity. New Engl J Med, 303;130-5

Giniger S et al (1983) Age, experience and performance on speed and skill jobs in an applied setting. Journal of Applied Psychology, 68;469-75

Goddard E (1991) Drinking in England and Wales in the late 1980s. OPCS, HMSO, London

Gordon SL, Corbin SB (1992) Summary of workshop on drinking water fluoride influence on hip fracture and bone health. Osteoporosis International 2:109-17

Gray JAM (1987) Education for health in old age in Prevention of diseases in the elderly, ed JAM Gray, Churchill Livingstone, London

Grimley Evans J (1985) Risk factors for stroke in the elderly. University of Cambridge, MD Dissertation

Grimley Evans J (1986) The decline of stroke. in Stroke: epidemiological, therapeutic and socioeconomic aspects, ed FC Rose, Royal Society of Medicine, London

Grimley Evans J (1987) Blood pressure and stroke in an elderly English population. J Epidemiol Community Health, 41;275-82

Grimley Evans J (1992) From plaque to placement; a model for Alzheimer's disease. Age Ageing, 21;77-80

Gruenberg EM (1977) The failures of success. Millbank Mem Fund Q, 55;3-24

Haggard M, Gatehouse S, Davis A (1981) The high prevalence of hearing disorders and its implications for services in the UK. British Journal of Audiology, 15;241-51.

Hagnell O, Lanke J, Rorsman B, Öhmann R, Öjesjö L (1983) Current trends in the incidence of senile and multi-infarct dementia. A prospective study of a total population followed over 25 years. The Lundby Study. Arch Psychiatr Nervenkr, 233;423-38

Hales CN, Barker DJP, Clark PMS et al (1991) Fetal and infant growth and impaired glucose tolerance at age 64. Br Med J, 303;1019-22

Harlow, S. D. et al (1991) A longitudinal study of risk factors for depressive symptomatology in elderly widowed and married women. American Journal of Epidemiology, 134;526-38

Herbst KG, Humphrey C (1980) Hearing impairment and mental status in the elderly living at home. British Medical Journal, 281;903-5.

Herbst KG et al (1991) Implications of hearing impairment for elderly people in London and in Wales. Acta Otolaryngologica, 476(Suppl);209-14.

Hill RD, Storandt M, Simeone C (1990) The effects of memory skills training and incentives on free recall in older learners. Journal of Gerontology: Psychological Sciences, 45;227-32

Hillbom M, Kaste M (1981) Ethanol intoxication a risk factor for ischaemic brain infarction in adolescents and young adults. Stroke, 12;422-5

Hoyer FW et al (1978) Training response speed in young and elderly women. International Journal of Aging and Human Development, 9;247-53

Huppert FA (1987) Cognitive function. in The Health and Lifestyle Survey, eds B Cox et al, Health Promotion Research Trust, London, pp43-50

Huppert FA et al (1987) Psychological Function. in The Health and Lifestyle Survey, eds B Cox et al, Health Promotion Research Trust, London

Jagger C, Clarke M, Cook AJ (1989) Mental and physical health of elderly people; five-year follow-up of a total population. Age Ageing, 18;77-82

Jarrett M, Shipley MJ and Rose G (1982) Weight and mortality in the Whitehall Study. British Medical Journal, 285;535-7

Jolleys JV (1988) Reported prevalence of urinary incontinence in women in a general practice. Brit Med J, 296;1300-2

Joossens JV (1973) Salt and hypertension, water hardness and cardiovascular disease. Triangle, 12;9-16.

Jorm AF (1990) The epidemiology of Alzheimer's disease and related disorders. Chapman and Hall, London

Katz S, Branch LG, Branson MH et al (1983) Active life expectancy. New Engl J Med, 309;1218-24

Kay DWK, Beamish P, Roth M (1964) Old age mental disorders in Newcastle upon Tyne. British Journal of Psychiatry, 110;146-58

Kay H (1951) Learning of a serial task by different age groups. Quarterly Journal of Experimental Psychology, 3;166-83

Kendell RE (1984a) The determinants of per capita consumption. In Alcohol; preventing the harm. Institute of Alcohol Studies, London, pp. 7-29

Kendell RE (1984b) The beneficial consequences of the UK's declining per capita consumption of alcohol in 1979-82. Alcohol and Alcoholism, 19;271-6

Kendell RE et al (1983) Effect of economic changes on Scottish drinking habits 1978-82. British Journal of Addiction, 78;365-79

Kline DW, Schieber F (1985) Vision and aging. in Handbook of the psychology of aging, 2nd ed. (eds. JE Birren and KW Schaie), Van Nostrand Reinhold, New York, pp.296-331.

Knight I (1984) The heights and weights of adults in Great Britain. HMSO, London

Krauss IK (1987) Reaction Time. in The encyclopedia of aging, ed GL Maddox, Springer, New York, pp557-558

LaCroix AZ, Wienpahl J, White LR, Wallace RB, Scherr PA, George LK, Cornoni-Huntley J, Ostfeld AM (1990) Thiazide diuretic agents and the incidence of hip fracture. New Engl J Med, 322;286-90

Law CM, Barker DJP, Bull AR, Osmond C (1991) Maternal and fetal influences on blood pressure. Arch Dis Childhood, 66;1291-5

Law MR, Wald NJ, Meade TW (1991) Strategies for prevention of osteoporosis and hip fracture. Brit Med J, 303;453-9

Leeder SR, Corkhill R, Irwig LM, Holland WW, Colley JRT (1976) Influence of family factors on the incidence of lower respiratory illness during the first year of life. Br J Preventive and Social Med, 30;203-12

Leibowitz HM, Krueger DE, Maunder LR et al (1980) The Framingham eye study monograph. Surv Ophthalmol, 24(suppl);335-610

Lichenstein MJ et al (1985) Systolic and diastolic blood pressures as predictors of coronary heart disease mortality in the Whitehall Study. British Medical Journal, 291; 243-5

Lynn R, Hampson S (1986) The rise of national intelligence: evidence from Britain, Japan and the USA. Personality and Individual Differences, 7;23-32

MacMahon, Peto R, Cutler J et al (1990) Blood pressure, stroke, and coronary heart disease. Part 1, prolonged differences in blood pressure; prospective observational studies corrected for regression dilution bias. Lancet, 335;765-74

Manton KG (1988) A longitudinal study of functional change and mortality in the United States. J Gerontol, 43;S153-61

Marmot MG et al (1981) Alcohol and mortality; a U-shaped curve. Lancet, 2;580-3

Marmot MG, Mann JI (1987) Epidemiology of ischaemic heart disease. in Ischaemic heart disease, ed Fox KM, MTP Press, Lancaster, pp1-31

Marmot MG, McDowall ME (1986) Mortality decline and widening social inequalities. Lancet, 2;274-6

Martin J, Meltzer H, Elliot D (1988) OPCS surveys of disability in Gt Britain, report 1, The prevalence of disability among adults. HMSO, London

Martin J, White A, Meltzer H (1991) OPCS surveys of disability in Gt Britain, report 4, Disabled adults; services transport and employment. HMSO, London

Maynard A, O'Brien B (1982) Harmonisation policies in the European Community and alcohol abuse. British Journal of Addiction, 77;235-44

McLachlan DR, Dalton AJ, Kruck TP, et al (1991) Intramuscular desferrioxamine in patients with Alzheimer's disease. Lancet, 337;1304-8

Meade TW, Chakrabarti R, Haines AP, North WRS, Stirling Y (1980) Haemostatic function and cardiovascular death; early results of a prospective study. Lancet, 1;1050-4

Melton LJ,III, Kan SJ, Frye MA, Wahner HW, O'Fallon WM, Riggs BL (1989) Epidemiology of vertebral fractures in women. Am J Epidemiol.129;1000-11

Menich SR, Baron A (1990) Age-related effects of reinforced practice on recognition memory: consistent versus varied stimulus response relations. Journal of Gerontology, 45;88-93

Miller PD, Neal BJ, McIntyre DO, Yanover MJ, Anger MS, Kowalski L (1991) Effect of cyclical therapy with phosphorus and etidronate on axial bone mineral density in postmenopausal osteoporotic women. Osteoporosis Int, 1;171-6

Mortimer JA, French LR, Hutton JT, Schuman LM (1985) Head injury as a risk factor for Alzheimer's disease. Neurology, 35;264-7

Murphy E (1982) Social origins of depression in old age. British Journal of Psychiatry, 141;135-142

Murrell S, Himmelfarb S, Wright K (1983) Prevalence of depression and its correlates in older adults. American Journal of Epidemiology, 117;173-85

National Fitness Survey (1992) – The Allied Dunbar National Fitness Survey – a report on activity patterns and fitness levels. The Sports Council and Health Education Authority, London

Oliver MF (1992) Doubts about preventing coronary heart disease. Br Med J, 304;393-4

OPCS (1981) The general household survey. HMSO, London

OPCS (1987) The general household survey. HMSO, London

OPCS (1988) General Household Survey. HMSO, London

OPCS (1988) The prevalence of disability among adults. OPCS surveys of disability in Great Britain. Report 1. OPCS, Social Survey Division, HMSO, London

OPCS (1990) The dietary and nutritional survey of British adults. HMSO, London

OPCS (1991) 1990 mortality statistics, cause, England and Wales. Series DH2 no;17, HMSO, London

OPCS (1991) Mortality statistics surveillance 1968-1985. Series DH1 no;22, HMSO, London

Osmond C, Barker DJP (1991) Ischaemic heart disease in England and Wales around the year 2000. J Epidemiol and Community Health, 45;71-2

Ouslander JG (1990) The efficacy of continence treatment. in Improving the health of older people; a world view, eds RL Kane, J Grimley Evans and D Macfadyen, Oxford University Press, Oxford

Oxford Regional Health Authority (1991) Lifestyle Survey. Oxford Regional Health Authority, Oxford

Parving A, Philip B (1991) Use and benefit of hearing aids in the tenth decade and beyond. Audiology, 30;61-9.

Popham RE, Schmidt W, de Lint J (1975) The prevention of alcoholism; epidemiological studies of the effect of government control measures. British Journal of Addiction, 70;125-44

Prince RL, Smith M, Dick IM, Price RI, Webb PG, Henderson NK, Harris MM (1991) Prevention of postmenopausal osteoporosis. A comparative study of exercise, calcium supplementation and hormone-replacement therapy. New Engl J Med, 325;1189-95

Prior IAM, Grimley Evans J, Davidson F, Lindsay M (1968) Sodium intake and blood pressure in two Polynesian populations. New Engl J Med, 279;515-20

Rabbitt P (1965) An age-decrement in the ability to ignore irrelevant information. Journal of Gerontology, 20;233-8

Rabbitt P (1983) How can we tell whether human performance is related to chronological age? in Aging of the brain, eds D Samuel et al, Raven Press, New York, pp9-18

Rabbitt P (1991a) Factors promoting accidents involving elderly pedestrians and drivers. in Behavioural research in road safety: proceedings of a seminar held at Nottingham University, eds GB Grayson and JF Lester, Transport and Road Research Laboratory, Crowthorne, Berkshire, pp167-183

Rabbitt P (1991b) Mild hearing loss can cause apparent memory failures which increase with age and reduce IQ. Acta Otolaryngologica (Stockholm) Supp 476:167-76

Rabbitt P (1992) Memory. in: Oxford textbook of geriatric medicine, ed J Grimley Evans and T Franklin Williams, Oxford University Press, Oxford

Ray WA, Griffin MR, Downey W, Melton LJ,III (1989) Long-term use of thiazide diuretics and risk of hip fracture. Lancet 1;687-90.

Registrar General's Statistical Returns for England and Wales (1962-1972) – Part I Tables, Medical. (1964-1974) HMSO, London

Reid DS, Grimley Evans J (1970) New drugs and changing mortality from non-infectious disease. Brit Med Bull, 26;191-6

Rhodes SR (1983) Age-related differences in work attitudes and behavior: a review and conceptual analysis. Psychological Bulletin, 93;328-67

RNID (1988) Hearing aids the case for change. Royal National Institute for the Deaf, London

Road Accidents of Great Britain (1990) The casualty report. HMSO, London

Robine JM, Colvez A, Bucquet D et al (1986) L'esperance de vie sans incapacite en France en 1982. Population (Paris), 41;1025-42

Robine JM, Ritchie K (1991) Healthy life expectancy; evaluation of global indicator of change in population health. Brit Med J, 302;457-60

Robinson RJ (1992) Is the child father of the man? Br Med J, 304;789-90

Rogers A, Rogers RG, Branch LG (1989) A multistate analysis of active life expectancy. Public Health Reports, 104;222-6

Royal College of Physicians (1962) Smoking and health; summary of a report on smoking in relation to cancer of the lung and other diseases. Pitman, London

Royal College of Physicians (1971) Smoking and health now; 2nd Report. Pitman, London

Royal College of Physicians (1977) Smoking or health; 3rd report. Pitman, London

Royal College of Physicians (1983) Obesity. Journal of the Royal College of Physicians, 17;5-65

Royal College of Physicians (1992) Preventive Medicine. London, Royal College of Physicians, p55-68

Salthouse TA (1984) Effects of age and skill in typing. Journal of Experimental Psychology: General, 113;345-71

Salthouse TA (1985) A theory of cognitive aging. North Holland, Amsterdam

Salthouse TA (1990) Cognitive competence and expertise in aging. in Handbook of the psychology of aging, 3rd ed, eds JE Birren and KW Schaie), Academic Press, San Diego, pp310-319

Schaie KW (1974) Transitions in gerontology – from lab to life: intellectual functioning. American Psychologist, 29;802-7

Schaie KW (1988) Ageism in psychological research. American Psychologist, 41;179-83

Schaie KW (1990) Intellectual development in adulthood. in Handbook of the psychology of aging, 3rd ed, eds JE Birren and KW Schaie, Academic Press, San Diego, CA, pp291-309

Schaie KW, Strother CR (1968) A cross-sequential study of age changes in cognitive behavior. Psychological Bulletin, 70;671-80

Schaie KW, Willis SL (1986) Can decline in adult intellectual functioning be reversed? Developmental Psychology, 22;223-32

Semple BM, Yarrow A (1974) Health education, alcohol and alcoholism in Scotland. Health Bulletin, 30;31-4

Shaper AG et al (1988) Alcohol and mortality in British men; explaining the U-shaped curve. Lancet, 2;1267-73

Shaper AG, Phillips AN, Pocock SJ, Walker M, Macfarlane PW (1991) Risk factors for stroke in middle aged British men. Brit Med J, 302;1111-5

Shaper AG, Wannamethee G (1991) Physical activity and ischaemic heart disease in middle-aged British men. Br Heart J, 66;384-94

Shephard RJ (1986) Fitness of a nation – the Canada Fitness Survey. Karger, Basel

Shephard RJ (1987) Physical Activity and Aging (Second Edition) Croom Helm, London

Shooter AMN et al (1956) Some field data on the training of older people. Occupational Psychology, 30;204-15

Skelton DA, Greig CA, Davies JM, Young A (1992) Muscle Strength in Healthy Men aged 65-84 Presented at British Geriatrics Society Spring Meeting, Swansea 1992. Abstract in press

Smart RG (1974) The effect of licensing restriction during 1914-1918 on drunkenness and liver cirrhosis deaths in Britain. British Journal of Addiction, 69;109-21

Sobonya RE, Burrows B (1983) The epidemiology of emphysema. Clinics in Chest Medicine, 4;351-8

Social Policy Research Unit (1989) Beyond plastic pants;-improving care for incontinence sufferers. DHSS 560 5/89 TH. Heslington, University of York, York

Spector TD, Cooper C, Fenton Lewis A (1990) Trends in admission for hip fracture in England and Wales, 1968-85. Brit Med J, 300;173-4

Steering Committee of the Physicians' health study research group (1989) Final report on the aspirin component of the ongoing physicians' health study. N Eng J Med, 321;129-35

Stephens SDG et al (1990) Hearing disability in people aged 50-65: effectiveness and acceptability of rehabilitative intervention. British Medical Journal, 300;508-11.

Storm T, Thamsborg G, Steiniche T, Genant HK, Sorensen OH (1990) Effect of intermittent cyclical etidronate therapy on bone mass and fracture rate in women with postmenopausal!osteoporosis. New Engl J Med, 322;1265-71

The Boston Area Anticoagulation Trial for Atrial Fibrillation Investigators (1990) The effect of low-dose warfarin on the risk of stroke in patients with nonrheumatic atrial fibrillation. New Engl J Med, 323;1505-11

The Stroke Prevention in Atrial Fibrillation Investigators (1991) Stroke prevention in atrial fibrillation study. Final results. Circulation, 84;527-39

Thomas A, Herbst KG (1980) Social and psychological implications of acquired deafness for adults of employment age. British Journal of Audiology, 14;76-85.

Thomas TM, Egan M, Walgrove A, Meade TW (1984) The prevalence of faecal and double incontinence. Comm Med, 6;216-20

Thomas TM, Plymat KR, Blannin J, Meade TW (1980) Prevalence of urinary incontinence. Brit Med J, 281;1243-5

Townsend J (1988) Costs of incontinence. Comm Med, 10;235-9

Turner RJ, Noh S (1988) Physical disability and depression. Journal of Health and Social Behavior, 29;23-37

Verbrugge LM (1984) Long life but worsening health? Trends in health and mortality of middle aged and older persons. Millbank Mem Fund Q, 62;475-519

Verrillo RT, Verrillo V (1985) Sensory and perceptual performance. In Aging and human performance (ed. N. Charness), John Wiley, Chichester, pp1-46

Vuori I, Suurnakki L, Suuranakki T (1982) Risk of sudden cardiovascular death in exercise. Medicine and Science in Sports and Exercise, 14;114-15

Wald NJ, Frost CD, Law MR (1991) By how much does dietary salt reduction lower blood pressure? Brit Med J, 302;818-24

Wald N, Nicolandes-Bowman A (1990) UK Smoking statistics, 2nd edition. Oxford University Press, Oxford

Wallace WA, Price VH, Elliot CA, MacPherson MBA, Scott BW (1990) Hormone replacement therapy acceptability to Nottingham post-menopausal women with a risk factor for osteoporosis. J Roy Soc Med, 83;699-701.

Wannamethee G, Shaper AG (1989) Body weight and mortality in middle aged British men; impact of smoking. British Medical Journal, 299;1497-502

Watts NB et al (1990) Intermittent cyclical etidronate treatment of postmenopausal osteoporosis. New Engl J Med, 323;73-9

Weale R (1989) Eyes and age. in Human ageing and later life: multidisciplinary perspectives (ed. AM Warnes). Edward Arnold, London, pp.38-46.

Welford AT (1976) Thirty years of psychological research on age and work. Journal of Occupational Psychology, 49;129-38

Welford AT (1988) Preventing adverse changes of work with age. International Journal of Aging and Human Development, 27;283-91

Whelton PK, Klag MJ (1989) The epidemiology of high blood pressure. Clinics in Geriatric Medicine, 5;639-55

Whisnant JP (1984) The decline of stroke. Stroke, 15;160-8

Wilcox RG (1991) Coronary thrombolysis; round two and beyond. Br Heart J, 65;175-6

Wilkinson RT, Allison S (1989) Age and simple reaction time: decade differences for 5,323 subjects. Journal of Gerontology, 4;29-35

Williams ME (1984) A quantitative method of identifying older persons at risk for increasing long term care services. Journal of Chronic Diseases, 37;705-711

Williams ME (1987) Identifying the older person likely to require long term care services. Journal of the American Geriatrics Society, 35;751-768

Winner SJ, Morgan CA, Grimley Evans J (1989) Perimenopausal risk of falling and incidence of distal forearm fracture. Brit Med J, 298;1486-8

Wolf PA, Abbott RD, Kannel WB (1987) Atrial fibrillation; a major contributor to stroke in the elderly. The Framingham study. Arch Int Med, 147;1561-4

Wormald RPL, Wright LA, Courtney P, Beaumont B, Haines AP (1992) Visual problems in the elderly population and implications for services. Br Med J, 304;1226-9

Young A (1986) Exercise physiology in geriatric practice. Acta Med Scand, 711(suppl);227-32

Zandri E, Charness N (1989) Training older and younger adults to use software. Educational Gerontology, 15;615-31